Thomas Thellusson Carter

The Doctrine of the Priesthood in the Church of England

Second Edition

Thomas Thellusson Carter

The Doctrine of the Priesthood in the Church of England
Second Edition

ISBN/EAN: 9783337260668

Printed in Europe, USA, Canada, Australia, Japan

Cover: Foto ©Lupo / pixelio.de

More available books at **www.hansebooks.com**

THE DOCTRINE OF THE PRIESTHOOD
IN THE
CHURCH OF ENGLAND.

THE DOCTRINE OF THE PRIESTHOOD

IN THE CHURCH OF ENGLAND.

BY

THOMAS THELLUSSON CARTER, M.A.,

RECTOR OF CLEWER.

Second Edition, revised.

LONDON:
JOSEPH MASTERS, ALDERSGATE STREET,
AND NEW BOND STREET.
MDCCCLXIII.

TO HIS BRETHREN

THE MEMBERS OF THE CLERICAL SOCIETY

IN

THE DEANERIES OF BURNHAM AND BRAY,

IN THE DIOCESE OF OXFORD,

THESE PAGES ARE AFFECTIONATELY INSCRIBED,

IN THANKFULNESS FOR HAVING BEEN TAUGHT BY THEM

HOW MUCH UNITY OF EARNEST FAITH

LINGERS STILL AMIDST OUR MANY DIVISIONS,

AND HOW EVEN VARIETIES OF OPINION BECOME VALUABLE LESSONS

OF HUMILITY, FORBEARANCE, AND MUTUAL KINDNESS.

CONTENTS.

CHAPTER I.
THE PRESBYTER VIEW OF THE MINISTRY 1

CHAPTER II.
THE ETYMOLOGY OF THE TERM PRIEST 7

CHAPTER III.
THE HISTORY OF THE TERM PRIEST IN THE ENGLISH CHURCH, FROM THE TIME OF THE REFORMATION 13

CHAPTER IV.
THE CONTRAST BETWEEN THE ENGLISH AND FOREIGN REFORMATIONS 23

CHAPTER V.
THE COMMISSION AND FUNCTIONS OF THE PRIESTHOOD IN THE CHURCH OF ENGLAND 30

CHAPTER VI.
TESTIMONY OF THE POST-APOSTOLIC CHURCH, OR THE PERIOD SUBSEQUENT TO THE FIRST CENTURY OF CHRISTIANITY . 52

CHAPTER VII.

TESTIMONY OF THE APOSTOLIC AGE, OR FIRST CENTURY OF CHRISTIANITY 69

CHAPTER VIII.

TESTIMONY OF THE HOLY SCRIPTURES 75

CHAPTER IX.

THE PRINCIPLE OF PRIESTHOOD 96

CHAPTER X.

ARGUMENT OF THE EPISTLE TO THE HEBREWS . . 108

CHAPTER XI.

REASONS WHY THE TERM ἹΕΡΕΎΣ (PRIEST) IS NOT APPLIED TO THE CHRISTIAN MINISTRY IN THE NEW TESTAMENT . . 118

CHAPTER XII.

OF THE TERMS "IMPROPER," "SPIRITUAL," ETC., AS APPLIED TO THE PRIESTHOOD AND ITS SERVICES 129

CHAPTER XIII.

THE CONNECTION BETWEEN THE CHURCH AND THE SYNAGOGUE 137

CHAPTER XIV.

THE PRIESTHOOD OF THE PEOPLE 146

CHAPTER XV.

THE CHIEF FUNCTION OF THE MINISTERIAL PRIESTHOOD . 155

APPENDIX 165

INTRODUCTION.

TWO different views are held of the meaning of the name, and of the character of the ministry, of a Priest. They may be distinguished as the Presbyter, and the Sacerdotal view. As one or other prevails, an entirely different idea of the Church system is the result. On a question important, not merely for its own sake, but in its connection also with other kindred doctrines, especially with the whole sacramental system of the Church, as well as many practical details of the spiritual life, it is of great moment to ascertain what the Church teaches. Our inquiry is limited to the doctrine of the Church of England on the point in question; but inasmuch as the Church of England refers to Holy Scripture, and the early undivided Church, for the groundwork of its judgments, and the meaning, whenever doubtful, of its rules and services, it becomes necessary to extend the scope of the argument, so as to embrace the records of antiquity and the Word of God.

The line proposed to be pursued is, first to state the Presbyter view, together with the authority on which it rests, and then to contrast with it what the writer believes to be the uniformly fixed, and only possible Church view of the question. The conclusions to be gathered from the teaching of the Church of England will first be considered, and afterwards the traditions of the Catholic Church, and the revelations of the Holy Scriptures. In conclusion, some considerations will be offered as to the principles of a priestly ministry, and an answer to certain leading objections which are commonly taken against the existence of such a ministry in the Christian Church.

An apology is needed for venturing to deal with a question on which such men as Thorndike and Hickes, &c., have written with so much learning;[1] but different ages require different modes of advocating the same truths, and the labours of former ages give facilities to those who would otherwise have been incompetent for the task. The necessity of a renewed study of the question, moreover, must be evident to any one who considers the religious controversies and doubts which

---

[1] Of the Government of Churches: a Discourse pointing at the Primitive Form. (1641.) Of Religious Assemblies, and the Public Service of GOD: a Discourse according to Apostolical Rule and Practice. (1642.) By Herbert Thorndike, sometime Prebendary of the Collegiate Church of S. Peter, Westminster.

The Christian Priesthood. (1695.) By George Hickes, D.D., sometime Fellow of Lincoln College, and Dean of Worcester.

perplex thoughtful persons in the present day; and if what is here brought forward should lead any, anxious for the truth, to search more deeply into the mysteries of the kingdom of GOD, or to see more clearly their own personal interest in them, the writer of these pages requests of such persons to overlook his great deficiencies in treating upon so momentous a subject, and to pray for him, that, after having thus expressed his convictions of the unearthly powers of the ministry in which he bears a part, he may not "himself be a castaway."

THE DOCTRINE OF THE PRIESTHOOD.

CHAPTER I.

THE PRESBYTER VIEW OF THE MINISTRY.

THE Presbyter view of the ministry rests chiefly on etymological considerations. The argument may be thus shortly stated. Priest is the abbreviated form of Presbyter, which is the term employed in Holy Scripture, to denote the second order of the Christian ministry. Presbyter, or Elder, is the name of an officer of the Jewish Synagogue. Therefore the term Priest implies what that office comprehended. The description of the Priestly office, when viewed according to this theory, embraces teaching, discipline, and generally the administration of religious rites and ceremonies. It is assumed that this combination of offices corresponds with the functions of the Jewish Elder, and this correspondence is urged as a further proof of the supposed substantial identity of the two offices.

The etymological argument will be discussed in the next chapter. The argument from Scripture will be considered in a later stage of our inquiry. The descrip-

THE DOCTRINE OF THE PRIESTHOOD.

tion of the ministry of the Elder, and its correspondence with that of the Priest, is a separate question, and is alone considered here.

The chief offices of a Jewish Synagogue, consisted of the Ruler, the Elders, the Collector of Alms, and the Angel or Legate, a name given indifferently to the reciter of the prayers, or to the messenger employed on commissions, whether to proselytise, or to carry alms, &c. There was no special officer appointed to read or teach in the regular services. The custom was to invite any person present to officiate for the occasion.[1]

The Elders acted as assistants to the Ruler in the

---

[1] Dr. Jahn, in his "Manual of Biblical Antiquities," thus enumerates the officers of the Synagogue. (Sec. 371. Translated by J. C. Upham.)

I. The "Ruler of the Synagogue," who presided over the assembly and invited readers and speakers.

II. The "Elders of the Synagogue," who acted as counsellors of the Ruler, took part in its internal management, and punished transgressors of the laws.

III. The "Collectors of Alms," or Deacons.

IV. The "Servants of the Synagogue," who delivered the books to the readers, &c., and performed other subordinate offices.

V. The "Messenger or Legate of the Synagogue," who was sent from one synagogue to another to carry alms, or commissioned to propagate religious knowledge.

The "Synagogue Preacher" is an officer introduced in later times. In the time of CHRIST, the person who read, or preached, was selected for the occasion from among those present.

The person selected to recite the prayers was called the messenger (ἄγγελος), as well as the regular officer known by that name. He is called by the Jews of modern times the "synagogue singer," or cantilator.

The Jews anciently called those persons who, from their superior erudition, were capable of teaching in the synagogue, "shepherds, or pastors." They applied the same terms, in more recent times, to the elders and deacons.

management of the concerns of the Synagogue, in procuring readers or speakers, and in preserving Ecclesiastical discipline among the members. They had not, strictly speaking, any religious office. If an elder happened to be learned in the Scriptures, which was not necessarily the case, he might expound, as any other person present in the congregation; but such ministration was entirely accidental to his distinctive office. Teaching and saying prayers, were separate functions, discharged by other persons.

The supposed parallelism, therefore, between the functions of the Christian Presbyter and the Jewish Elder, does not hold good; the theory is forced to assume the combination of offices ordinarily kept distinct, as though they co-existed in one person. The question at issue is as to the distinctive character of one—the second order—of the Apostolic ministry, and the Presbyter theory proceeds on the assumption, that this order is represented by the officer bearing the *name* of Elder in the Jewish Synagogue. But in drawing the comparison of their respective functions, the comparison is made to lie, not with the single office which the name properly represents, but with a combination of offices discharged by several different persons. In order to establish the theory, it is necessary to supplement the simple view of the Elder, who was properly only an Ecclesiastical Judge or magistrate, with the addition of a ministry of religion.

It is most important to bear this in mind, because the objection urged against the sacerdotal view of the Christian ministry is this, that it assumes the addition of elements of service incompatible with the original meaning of the term Presbyter; an objection which cannot be fairly urged by the upholders of the Presbyter view, inasmuch as their own theory likewise requires an addition of functions, not properly belonging to the proposed prototype. Both the Presbyter and the sacerdotal views alike assume the addition of elements which the office of the Jewish Elder did not represent. The only question between the two theories, therefore, regards the *amount* of addition to the meaning of the original term, not to the principle of addition in itself.

The Presbyter theory is based mainly on the authority of Vitringa, a Dutch Presbyterian of the last century,[1] though it did not originate with him. The theory was advanced first by Grotius, his fellow-countryman, also a Presbyterian, from whom it was adopted by Selden, a lay-elder in Cromwell's Council of Divines. Vitringa appeals to these two writers in support of his views; he also adduces, among English divines, the respected names of Thorndike and Lightfoot, as authorities favourable to his theory. In referring however to Thorndike, Vitringa omits to state, that while the writer mentions the resemblance existing between the Christian minister and the Jewish Elder, he asserts at the same time the yet closer correspondence between him and the Jewish Priest. Nor does Vitringa explain that Thorndike uses the term Synagogue in its widest sense, including the entire Jewish economy.

It is of the utmost importance to distinguish the two-

---

[1] Vitringa took his Doctor's degree in Divinity, at the University of Leyden, in 1759. The book referred to, is his treatise, "De Synagogâ Vetere."

fold sense of the term Synagogue, which means sometimes the entire Jewish system, sometimes the special place of assembly. Unless this distinction is clearly kept in view, the mere mention of the term may appear to favour the Presbyter view, when in reality the author may be tracing the Christian ministry to a very different part of the Jewish system. Bishop Andrewes e.g. employs the term in its wider sense in his "Summary View of the Government of the Old and New Testament," where he is tracing the correspondence exclusively between the Christian minister and the Jewish Priest.

When referring to Lightfoot, Vitringa, with a naïve simplicity, acknowledges this fact of the double meaning of the term, and Lightfoot's use of it in its wider sense, thus contradicting the apparent support which he claims. "It cannot be dissembled, that this learned man uses the word Synagogue in its widest acceptation, for the whole Jewish economy, including the Temple, as well as the Synagogue proper." Even in the passage which Vitringa quotes from Lightfoot, there occurs the mention of "Sacrifices, Priests, (sacerdotes), Deacons or Levites," as marks of correspondence between the two systems. Lightfoot and Thorndike are the only authorities of the English Church, whom Vitringa claims in support of his view.

The reasons which induce Vitringa to rest satisfied in this supposed derivation of the Christian ministry from the Jewish Synagogue, need to be considered in order to appreciate the weight of his authority. The following are the only reasons which he gives, and they occur in the order stated.[1]

[1] See Prolegomena, c. v.

1. A Synagogue might be built anywhere; the Temple only on one spot.

2. In the Synagogue there was no distinction of persons or ministers; any one present might be appointed to officiate for the occasion. In the Temple, only certain ordained persons could officiate. The same liberty, he adds, flourishes in our Churches.

3. In the worship of the Temple, a particular dress was required. In the Synagogue, an official dress was used, and there was even a slovenliness in this respect, (aliquando nimius etiam videri possit vestium esse neglectus).

4. There was greater liberty in regard to the age of those who officiated in the Synagogue.

5. Some minute points are enumerated, as e.g. that no one maimed in body could be a Priest, but he could officiate in the Synagogue.

6. The Temple had its gradations among its ministers, (sanctitatis religione gradus,) its altars, vessels, furniture, &c., but they are wanting in the Synagogue and the Church.

7. The Temple worship consisted more of sacrifices, benedictions, &c.; that of the Synagogue of congregational prayer.

It is evident from what point of view Vitringa looks at the question, and how he regards the Church. A real Churchman from *his* point of view, must have drawn a precisely opposite conclusion from every one of the same premises.

CHAPTER II.

THE ETYMOLOGY OF THE TERM PRIEST.

IT has been observed that the presbyter view of the Christian Ministry depends on the etymology of the term; the argument being that because Priest is the abbreviated form of presbyter, it consequently bears the same meaning, and implies the same kind of ministry. The consideration, therefore, of the etymological bearing of the question is of primary importance.

To trace the origin of a word in a foreign language, and under a foreign system, from whence it has been transferred many hundred years ago, must always be an uncertain method of ascertaining its meaning in current use. Words are not fossils, which, transplanted from one bed of matter to another, preserve their primæval forms from age to age; but rather like fluid atoms they are ever running into fresh shapes and combinations. When transferred, they come into contact with new ideas, and then become representatives of those new ideas. They are as true representatives of the new ideas to which they are thenceforward attached, as they were before of the ideas which previously belonged to them; for words are mere conventional representatives of whatever the creative mind chooses to express by their means. They are the "counters" of thought, and are changed about at will, now standing for one, now for another combination of ideas. This happens more or less in the case of every transferred word, for no two nations, or two systems are precisely alike, and the more pregnant with meaning, the more vitally associated with the interests of humanity any term may be, the deeper is the new impression stamped upon it.

Terms of religion, beyond all other terms, are liable to be changed in their meanings, because they are associated with ideas which touch upon the deepest springs of thought, and are symbols of the outgoings of the Infinite. And the deeper the revelations which any religion contains, the more sure it is that the terms it borrows from other sources will be clothed in the transference with new and greater mysteries. What notion, e.g., would be obtained of the word Bishop, by simply referring a student to its etymological meaning, "overseer?" Apostle, again, was the name of a subordinate officer of the Sanhedrim, and S. Paul held this office, when he was charged with letters to Damascus, to destroy the disciples of our LORD. But who could discern any resemblance between Saul starting from Jerusalem for Damascus, and S. Paul traversing Asia Minor, or standing on Mars' hill? What notion of a Sacrament could one have, on being taught that the word among the ancient Romans meant a regimental oath; or of Holy Baptism, by learning that it etymologically meant washing by water? That, like to these and all other transferred words, Priest has changed its meaning, and now truly represents the same idea, which was conveyed of old, among the Hebrews by Cohen, among the Greeks by ἱερεύς, among the Romans by Sacerdos, and among the Gothic nations by Gudi, is only one instance of an universal law.

Moreover, the synonymous words in the ancient languages underwent in their day precisely the same change, as is here supposed to have happened to the term Presbyter. 'Cohen' originally meant, according to some authorities, 'one who ministers or transacts business for another,' or, as in the margin of our Bible (Gen. xli. 45), 'a prince,' or as Simoni, comparing it with its corresponding Arabic root, prefers, 'a prophet.' Ἱερεύς, Sacerdos, and Gudi, (from Gud or God,) meant simply, 'one employed about holy things.' The distinctive attributes of Priesthood were superadded to the original meanings of those words, in consequence of their association with the special doctrines and offices of religion, which by common use they came to represent.[1]

The term Presbyter has itself undergone many changes. Originally denoting an elder by birth, like 'senator' among the Romans, it had before the time of Moses acquired the meaning of a ruler or judge. It is used in the Pentateuch and the historical books of the Old Tes-

[1] The term Priest (ἱερεύς) does not appear in the Bible, till it is applied to Aaron and his sons, (except in reference to Melchisedek, Potipherah, and Jethro), and yet there was a Priesthood in the Patriarchal line from the time of the fall, when sacrifices were first instituted. It does not clearly appear what name was used to denote the office. Perhaps the term 'Prophet' was so used, as in Gen. xx. 7, where the act of intercession spoken of is a priestly act. This gives countenance to Simoni's explanation of the etymology of Cohen. The union of the offices of Priest and Prophet appears to have been common in patriarchal times, and the exercise of the priestly office by prophets, as by Samuel (1 Sam. ix. 13, and xiii. 13), and by Nathan (2 Sam. xii. 13), even under the Mosaic law, is probably a lingering prolongation of patriarchal customs.

tament, to denote indifferently ecclesiastical or civil authority. We read of the "elders of the people," the "elders of every city," the "elders of the Priests," as well as the "elders" of the Synagogue. It was a lay, not a clerical term. In the language of the Apostles "elder" became the name of a minister of religion, and it underwent another change when the Apostolic Fathers of the first century selected it as the technical appellation of the second order of the Christian ministry, contrasted with Bishop and Deacon. Through this association, as in the case of the ancient names above mentioned, it then acquired the meaning of a sacerdotal office exercised by that order in the Church.

As Christianity spread in the West, Presbyter was adopted in the native languages, and became in Germany, 'Priester;' in France, 'Prêtre;' in Spain, 'Presbytero;' in England, 'Priest;' and these words in the Western Church, were used synonymously with 'sacerdote' in Italy and Spain; ἱερεύς in the East (in modern Greek pronounced 'ée-e-reffs'); 'Hieree' or 'Sviâshennick,' i.e., one consecrated, in Russia; 'Kamanaij,' i.e., one who sacrifices, in Armenia; 'sagart,' (pronounced saggurt,) from 'sacerdos,' in Ireland, and offeiriadd, offerer, in Welsh.[1]

The philological argument is very remarkable. In

---

[1] An uniform law, worthy of notice, has guided the mind of the Church in the choice of appropriate names for the priesthood. One or more names have been employed officially, and are found in the Service books; other names implying reverence, but of a more familiar kind, have been used in colloquial language. The names given in the text are the official and more solemn appellations. The following are the familiar terms which have been employed:—In the East, 'Papas,' father; in Russia, 'Pope,' evidently derived from Papas, or 'Batushka,' my dear

the East πρεσβύτερος existed as the appellation of the second order in the ministry, long enough to give rise to its many derivatives in the West, and then gradually fell out of use. The term passed into the West impressed with the idea of ἱερεύς; for the German, French and English languages have no term to represent a sacerdotal ministry, except the derivatives from presbyter, and these derivatives have been used in intimate association with that idea from the earliest period of the Christian life of those nations. This association is proved by the prevailing use of sacerdos in the service-books of the Western Church, as of ἱερεύς in those of the East. The name and idea of sacerdos was so established in the West at the time when Ireland was Christianised, as to furnish the derivative, sagart, without any trace of the Presbyter in name or idea. The Church thus sealed the derivatives of πρεσβύτερος with its sanction, as fitted to be used indifferently with the ancient sacerdotal terms and their derivatives.

It becomes evident, therefore, that the etymology of

father, the more respectful term; in Italy and Spain, 'Padre;' in France, 'Père;' in Germany, 'Geistlicht,' ghostly man.

The custom of the English Church is strictly according to Catholic rule. When Sacerdos was the title in the office books, Priest was the colloquial term. But when, on the translation of the Service books, Priest became the official title, another term was required for familiar use, and Clergyman, an ancient name derived from κλῆρος, 'the lot of the LORD,' as opposed to λαός, 'the people of the LORD,' and meaning, therefore, 'one of the sacred lot,' was adopted for common use. A remarkable instinct rules the minds of men, even when ignorant of the principle at stake, and perhaps even opposed to it. Scarcely any one would use the term Clergyman, except of a minister of the Church of England. Terms such as 'minister,' 'pastor,' which have no distinctive meaning, are employed to designate religious teachers out of the Church, thus marking the want of any distinctive or priestly character.

the term, Priest, is no guide to its interpretation, and that the long-sanctioned usage of the term has become its real, and only true meaning. If this be not the case, it lies with objectors to account for two striking phenomena; (1) how it happened that modern Europe, in the formation of some of its chief languages, should have failed to produce words representing an idea so well known, and so universal. And (2), what involves a far more serious question, how the Church, notwithstanding its subtle elaboration of the Creeds, and accurate distinctions of theological phrases on all disputed points of doctrine, should in this case have gone on using a misnomer, "deceiving and being deceived." This latter supposition is a necessary consequence of the presbyter view, and it attributes to the Church a want of distinction in language which could not fail to produce a lamentable and most injurious want of distinction in thought. Another, and surely the more probable conclusion is, that neither those nations of modern Europe, nor the Church, needed to coin another word, simply because this transferred term, following the common law of language affecting all borrowed words, had with sufficient certainty acquired the meaning which needed to be expressed.

We are in truth dealing not with words, but with things; with a living reality which is daily revealing itself in acts of unearthly power and benediction to all them that believe. And the true mode of ascertaining the meaning of the word Priest consequently must be, by considering the ideas which it actually represents, and the nature of the ministry which by common consent it designates.

CHAPTER III.

THE HISTORY OF THE TERM PRIEST IN THE ENGLISH CHURCH, FROM THE TIME OF THE REFORMATION.

WE are naturally led to the Reformation as the crisis, at which the mind of the Church of England upon the point in question was specially manifested. For the Service Books at that period being translated into the mother tongue, the Church was free to select the most suitable term, as the designation of the officiating minister.

Sacerdos had been in use in the Latin Service Books up to the time of the Reformation, and Priest was the familiar term to express its meaning. This term had become fixed in the mind and conscience of the people of England, as the only native word to denote a sacerdotal ministry. If it had been the purpose of the Reformers to reject the ideas universally attached to the name, they must of necessity have abandoned the name itself. And there were other names ready to their hand. They might have employed throughout the Prayer Book, as they did in some places, the term Minister or Pastor, then, as now, the favourite appellations of the foreign Reformers: or, taking the language of Scripture as their rule, they might have used the unabbreviated term, Presbyter. When, on the contrary, they adopted the term, Priest, of the meaning of which at the time there could be no doubt, they must have intended to preserve also the ideas attached to it. Having enshrined the popular term in the sacred books of the Church, they could not have expected the ideas, which it represented, to die out, or that the people would go back for its interpretation to Jewish times and the usage of the synagogue.

It cannot be urged that the English Reformers acted in this matter blindly, and without consideration of the grave questions involved. The Presbyterians at the same time rejected the term, Priest, simply because of the popular ideas attached to it. Moreover, the tendency of the English Reformers was to go to the extremest limit of conciliation, in hopes of winning as many as possible to unite in one common cause. No greater instance of this tendency can be given, than the removal of the term, Altar, from the Prayer Book. The term was used throughout the first Prayer Book of Edward VI.; it disappears from the second.[1] Though its removal is deeply to be regretted, yet there was no real change of doctrine involved, for where there is a Priest, there must needs be an altar; and the terms altar and holy table were indifferently used by the Fathers. To have retained the term, Priest, under such circumstances, is the more striking, and must be regarded as an unmistakeable testimony to the conviction of our

---

[1] The term 'altar' remains in use in the Coronation Service as well as in several Acts of Parliament (see Dr. Phillimore's speech on the appeal of Liddell *versus* Westerton, in the case of SS. Paul and Barnabas); and also prevails universally in the mind and familiar language of the people.

Reformers, that while some popular errors had to be corrected, no change was needed in this respect.

But besides the pressure against the use of this term, arising from the Ultra-Reformers, the question was thoroughly mooted between the English Divines and the advocates of the Church of Rome. There were warm disputes at the time as to the validity of our ordinations, whether or no our Clergy possessed full sacerdotal powers. If sacerdotal powers had not been claimed by the advocates of the English Reformation, the argument would have been at an end. But the assertion of the validity of our ordinations, as involving such powers, was peculiarly strong and decided. "I answer again," says Archbishop Bramhall, "that in our very essential form of priestly ordination, priestly power and authority is sufficiently expressed. We need not seek for a needle in a bottle of hay. The words of our ordinal are clear enough." (Discourse v. 486.) The question turned on the doctrine of the Eucharistic Sacrifice, and the Real Presence in the Blessed Sacrament. The line of the discussion may be gathered from Bramhall's treatises, and the writings of Bishop Andrewes.[1] Taking their statements as our guide, we learn that the question was, not as to the truth of these mysterious doctrines, on which both parties were agreed, but as to the mode of defining them. The Church of England advocates opposed the particular definition of doctrine,

---

[1] Bramhall and Andrewes were the two great writers, who during the reigns of Elizabeth and James I., when the principles of the English Reformation had attained a settled form, conducted the controversy with the Church of Rome, the former against the Bishop of Chalcedon, the latter against Cardinal Bellarmine.

known by the term, Transubstantiation, and whatever might be strictly consequent upon that definition; but they were willing to accept any form of explanation which had the warrant of Holy Scripture, and a true Catholic tradition. They only rejected words which implied the denial of the true existence of the symbols of bread and wine after consecration, or any idea of a repetition of the Sacrifice of the Cross, or a sacrifice of the same kind. They sought to preserve the idea of a Sacrifice commemorative of the Sacrifice of the Cross, pleading and obtaining its merits, under the symbols of bread and wine, and to cast around the consecrated elements the veil of the simpler faith of early days; not seeking to define too minutely the manner of the Divine operation, content to adore a Presence of the Incarnate GOD in intimate association with the elements, but according to supernatural laws of being, which no logical description could grasp, or human thought or language reduce to any known form.

The doctrine of the Sacrifice in the Holy Eucharist will come to be considered more fully in a later stage of the inquiry. It is only necessary now to observe the bearing of these discussions on the claim made by our Reformers to a true Priesthood, and how in retaining the name they intended to use it in a real sense according to the then prevailing view of priestly functions.

The following extracts from Archbishop Bramhall will show the mode in which that great writer, and other like defenders of the Reformation in England, met the charge of having lost a true Priesthood from the supposed denial of essential truth as to the doctrine of the Blessed Sacrament:

"We acknowledge," he says, "a Eucharistical sacrifice of praise and thanksgiving; a commemorative sacrifice, or a memorial of the Sacrifice of the Cross; a representative sacrifice, or a representation of the Passion of CHRIST before the eyes of His heavenly FATHER; an impetrative sacrifice, or an impetration of the fruits and benefits of His Passion, by way of real prayer; and, lastly, an applicative sacrifice, or an application of His merits unto our souls. Let him that dare, go one step further than we do, and say that it is a suppletory sacrifice, to supply the defects of the Sacrifice of the Cross; or else let them hold their peace and speak no more against us in this point of sacrifice for ever." (Discourse iii. sec. vi.)

In another passage Bramhall first states the objection of the advocates of Rome, and then answers it:

"The form, or words," said the Archbishop's opponents, "whereby men are made priests, must express authority and power to consecrate or make present CHRIST's Body and Blood (whether with or without Transubstantiation is not the present controversy with Protestants)." To which Bramhall replies: "Thus far we accord to the truth of the Presence of CHRIST's Body and Blood, so they leave us this latitude for the manner of His Presence. Abate us Transubstantiation, and those things which are consequent of this determination of the manner of Presence, and we have no difference with them in this particular.[1] They who are

[1] Bishop Andrewes gives the following answer to Bellarmine in terms precisely according with Bramhall:

"We believe a Real Presence no less than you; *concerning the mode of the Presence we define nothing rashly.*"

And again: "CHRIST said, 'This is My Body,' not 'This is My Body

ordained priests ought to have power to consecrate the Sacrament of the Body and Blood of CHRIST; that is, to make them present after such manner as they were present at the first institution, whether it be done by the enunciation of the words of CHRIST, as it is observed

in this mode.' We agree with you concerning the object; *all the dispute is concerning the mode* (de modo lis omnis est)."

And again: "De hoc est, fide firmâ tenemur quod sit; de hoc modo est, ut sit per, sive in, sive cum, sive sub, sive trans, nullum inibi verbum est." "We hold by a firm belief, that 'This' (the consecrated Bread) is the Body of CHRIST; of the manner how it is so, whether 'by,' or 'in,' or 'with,' or 'under,' or 'changeably with,' there is nothing said in the Scripture." (Casaubon, Epist. 393.)

Speaking generally, only one question on the subject of the Blessed Sacrament was agitating Christendom,—whether a Real Objective Presence of the Blessed Body and Blood of CHRIST was associated with the consecrated elements, or no; for the Zuinglian belief of a Presence to the soul of the worthy communicant cannot, in any true sense, be termed a Real Presence, as these words are theologically understood. The Roman, Lutheran, and English communions agreed in this main doctrine of the Real Objective Presence; the difference only regarded the manner. What the Church of England guarded against in denying Transubstantiation, is evident from the words of the Article. "Transubstantiation, or the *change of the substance* of bread and wine." The Real Objective Presence is left perfectly untouched by these words; neither is it denied that there is *a* change of the elements; only it is not a change of their *substance.*

Another idea, which had popularly grown up, was also guarded against, where it is said, at the close of the Eucharistic Office, "that no adoration is intended, or ought to be done, unto any *corporal* Presence of CHRIST's *natural* Flesh and Blood." These words were used to exclude the idea of a natural Presence after some *material* law of being. The terms are technical, and were employed to meet this peculiar popular idea, then, as it appears, current. But these words by no means affect the question of a Real Objective Presence after a heavenly manner suited to spiritual substances. "In the Supper of the LORD," as our Homily says, "is no vain ceremony, *no bare sign, no untrue figure of a thing absent,*" &c. (Sermon on Sacrament, First Part.)

by the Western Church, or by prayer, as it is practised in the Eastern Church, or whether these two be both the same things in effect; that is, that the form of Sacraments be mystical prayers and implicit invocations. Our Church for more abundant caution useth both these forms, as well in the consecration of the Sacrament, as in the ordination of priests." (Consecration of Protestant Bishops Vindicated. Discourse v. c. xi.)

After summing up the whole question, he dismisses it with the following brief and conclusive assertion:

" He who saith, Take thou authority to exercise the office of a priest in the Church of GOD (as the Protestant consecrators do), doth intend all things requisite to the priestly function, and among the rest, to offer a representative Sacrifice, to commemorate and apply the Sacrifice which CHRIST made upon the Cross."[1]

In the year 1662, a slight, though, as marking the anxiety with which the Church of England has sought to remove any doubt, or ground of opposition on this point, an important, change was made in our Ordination Service. The form of the commission originally stood simply thus: " Receive the HOLY GHOST: whose sins ye remit, they are remitted," &c. The advocates of Rome urged a defect, because the term Priest was not expressed. It was felt to be a captious objection; for the words in which our LORD had ordained the Apostles, and the words originally used in our Ordinal are but a simple repetition of them, could hardly with reason be deemed deficient. But in order to obviate any possible misapprehension, the term Priest was introduced, and

[1] Protestants' Ordination defended against the objection of S. N. Discourse vii. 3.

the form of the commission altered, as it now stands: "Receive the HOLY GHOST for the office and work of a Priest now committed to thee, by the imposition of our hands. Whose sins thou dost forgive," &c.

But at the Savoy Conference of this same year, held for the revision of the Prayer Book, the most striking and conclusive testimony was given of the deliberate judgment of the Church of England. There could be no doubt at this time as to the real question at issue between the Church and the Nonconformists. Priestcraft had been the loudest cry of the enemies of the Church during the reign of Charles I. It had heralded the way to the desecration of every altar in England, the suppression of the Prayer Book, and the prostration of the Church itself, which closed that disastrous period. The enemies of the priesthood and of the crown obtained their temporary triumph. The Presbyter had his day; and Cromwell's lay elders were the hierophants of the Great Rebellion. When therefore the Nonconformist divines asked the Bishops to remove the term Priest from the Prayer Book, and as minister was used in some, so it should be in all, places, the Bishops knew well what their request meant. As in a former generation, James I. coming out of Scotland, understood better than they in England the working of the presbyter theory, and expressed the results of a sorely won experience in his well known apothegm, "No Bishop, no King;" so the Bishops, who survived the Great Rebellion, must have learnt by a yet sadder experience, the truth which S. Jerome had expressed many years before in a corresponding apothegm, "No Priest, no

Church."[1] It is amusing, if we consider the recollections which must have been present to the minds of both parties in that eventful conference, to observe the quaint quietness and simplicity with which the Bishops put aside the request: "It is not reasonable," they said, "that the word minister should be only used in the Liturgy. For since some parts of the Liturgy may be performed by a deacon, others by none under the order of a priest, viz., absolution and consecration, it is fit that some such word as priest should be used for these offices, and not minister, which signifies at large every one that ministers in that holy office, of what order soever he be." (Cardwell's Documentary Annals, ch. vii. prop. ii.) The Nonconformists had better have left the matter alone. The Bishops, like Solomon when Queen Bathsheba pleaded for Adonijah, awakened to a quicker sense of impending danger, saw that there was no safety, except in the removal of the aspirant. They not only refused to displace the term Priest in favour of minister, but, on the contrary, introduced the term Priest in the stead of minister in two important places where doctrine was at stake, and entirely cast out the term pastor, the favourite appellation of the Nonconformists, from the only place in the Prayer Book where it seemed to challenge to itself a distinctive meaning. In the rubric before the Absolution, minister was displaced and Priest substituted; and in the Litany, the suffrage which had previously been for "Bishops, pastors, and ministers,"

[1] S. Hieron. adv. Lucif. c. 8. Ecclesia non est, quæ non habet Sacerdotes. (Where there is no Priesthood, there is no Church.) Quoted by Dr. Wordsworth. Theoph. Anglic. p. 214.

was changed into "Bishops, priests, and deacons."[1] It is impossible to conceive a more decisive proof of the mind of the Church of England. The question had come to a complete issue, with full knowledge of all the circumstances involved, and a powerful opposition in favour of the presbyter view. In the face of this opposition the Bishops decided, (and there was no dissentient voice among them,) to reject "minister," which, according to the presbyter view, is the correct term, and uphold "priest," which it condemns as unscriptural. In consequence of disagreements on this and other similar points of doctrine, the Nonconformists separated from the Church. Since that time the question has been at rest, and no occasion has been given to reassert these repeated decisions.[2]

[1] The term Pastor occurs twice, in the Collects for S. Matthias' and S. Peter's Day; but in both cases it is used in a general sense, as in Scripture.

[2] Among those who were appointed to conduct the Savoy conference, who thus decided the question as to the term Priest, may be mentioned Sheldon, Cosin, Morley, Sanderson, Walton, Gunning, Pearson, Sparrow, Thorndike.

It is more than a matter of curiosity to remark, that in the rubrics of the first Prayer Book of Edward VI.'s reign, the term Priest occurs ninety times; in those of the second, fifty-five times; in those of our present Prayer Book, eighty-eight times. It will be readily observed by any one who may investigate this Church usage, that the term is used on principle, and that wherever "Priest" is the term employed, more or less of sacerdotal authority is implied. The term, minister, on the contrary is used, where the office is simply ministerial, although this term also appears to have sometimes a specific meaning synonymous with Priest. See note, p. 46.

CHAPTER IV.

THE CONTRAST BETWEEN THE ENGLISH AND FOREIGN REFORMATION.

THE course pursued by the Church of England becomes clearer, when contrasted with that of the foreign Reformers. The choice of the terms, which they respectively adopted as the designation of the ministry, hinged upon the difference of their respective systems. It is therefore important to advert, though briefly, to the different principles of the contending parties.

The Reformation proceeded on three separate lines, readily distinguishable one from the other. In England the Bishops and Clergy combined in the movement. There was therefore no break in the Apostolic succession, and the grace of the Sacraments flowed on uninterruptedly. There was no change, and no temptation to change, in this respect. The Church system remained entire in all its vital elements, and with the same original powers of perpetuation.

It was not so abroad. No Bishop supported the Reformation in Germany. Luther was a Priest, and he was joined only by some of his own order. They continued, as before, to administer Sacraments, and taught their efficacy. The Confession of Augsburg, which embodies the principles of the German Reformation, asserts Regeneration in Baptism, private confession to a Priest, the grace of Absolution, and the Real Presence in the Holy Eucharist.[1] It also fully recognises the Priesthood (sacerdotium). What may be called the Church system, as a matter of mere doctrine, remained unchanged in the Lutheran scheme. The loss was of a practical kind. Without an episcopate, how was it possible to continue the succession? Luther, yielding to the necessities of his position, introduced the perfectly novel doctrine of Priests ordaining Priests. Thus a true sacramental system was retained, with true Priests to administer it for a time; but without the only ordained means of transmitting the same powers to the succeeding generation.

The Reformation assumed yet another phase in Switzerland. Calvin, its leader, was not in Priest's orders. He had, consequently, no authority to administer sacraments. The question in his case was, how to preserve Christianity without priesthood or sacraments. Influenced both by temper and position, he took the bold line of rejecting the traditionary doctrine of the Priesthood altogether. He taught that CHRIST alone is the Priest of the New Testament; that to attribute a Priesthood to any other, is a disparagement of our Blessed LORD, except so far as all Christians are called priests; and that Christian ministers are only what their

---

[1] See Dr. Pusey's notes to his sermon, lately published, in which he proves that the early Lutheran view of the Real Presence was identical with that of the Church of England; and that Consubstantiation, as it has been called, was a perversion of their creed, and not taught by the first Lutherans.

Scriptural names—presbyters, pastors, and teachers—denote.

These views are exhibited in detail in the Helvetic Confession, which contains the views of the Swiss Reformers, as the Confession of Augsburgh contains those of the German Reformers. Calvin accordingly instituted a new order of ministry, without any claim to sacerdotal powers. But how then to dispose of Sacraments? Calvin taught that they were signs symbolizing, not conveying, grace, though grace followed in the use of them by the elect. He thus separated the sign from the thing signified, making the one independent of the other. The outward elements, according to his view, only exhibit to the soul the truth of which they are the symbols, while the grace promised is to be sought, not through their instrumentality, but direct from heaven, and may be given or not, according to the conditions of the partaker. The difficulty still remaining was, how to ensure the promised grace, when Calvin's ministry laid no claim to a Divine commission, and, according to the universal tradition of the Church, the promises are ordinarily conveyed only through those who possess it. To obviate this difficulty, Calvin conceived and taught, that the faith of the receiver, not the act of consecration, is the instrumental cause of grace in sacraments.[1] Thus he constituted every man his

---

[1] Strong expressions are to be found in Calvin's writings as to the grace which may be received through the Holy Eucharist. And such passages may lead the reader to suppose that he harmonises with Catholic doctrine, unless he is careful to compare them with other statements which clearly shew that he considers the grace of GOD to depend only on the act of the mind stimulated by the outward symbol. Thus,

own priest. The Christian ministry accordingly became, in Calvin's system, nothing but an organ of government and instruction, which the term elder, the characteristic feature of Presbyterianism, sufficiently denotes.

History has shown the result of these two foreign systems. Presbyterianism, the bolder and more consistent, has lived. Having made no pretensions to a Divine commission, and formed independently of priestly ministrations, the Presbyterians, losing nothing in the lapse of time, have preserved unchanged the traditions of their founder. Calvinism is at this day a living and a powerful idea; though still, as at its commencement, essentially human in its organisation. Lutheranism, on the other hand, betrays the inevitable consequences of an inconsistent position; of an attempt to live without the means of life. With the Priests of Luther's generation died out the means of ministering sacraments; and with the reality the very idea and name of Priesthood gra-

---

e.g. he says, "CHRIST does not address the bread, to command it to become the Body, but enjoins His disciples to eat, and promises them the communication of His Body and Blood. Nor does Paul teach any other order than that the promises should be offered to the faithful, together with the bread and cup. And this is the truth. We are not to imagine any magical incantation, or think it sufficient to have muttered over the words, as if they were heard by the elements; but we are to understand these words, by which the elements are consecrated, to be a lively preaching, which edifies the hearers, which penetrates their minds, which is deeply impressed on their hearts, which exerts its efficacy in the accomplishment of that which it promises."—Inst. book iv., chap. 17. sec. 39.

Calvin evidently rejects the idea of an external objective Presence independent of the faith of the communicant, as well as the instrumentality of the consecrated elements in the conveyance of the gift.

dually disappeared. The Confession of Augsburg is no criterion of the Lutheranism of the present day. It is a remarkable instance of the true connection existing between the language and mind of a people, that while the Lutheran Priest has become the pastor, the term Bishop yet lives amongst them; the reason being, that while they have lost the idea of Priesthood, they have retained a quasi-episcopal form of church government. Such is the general case; though exceptions are to be found in the Scandinavian peninsula, and some remoter districts, where lingers still the semblance of an external religion, with the names of Priest, sacrament, and ritual.

The main difference, therefore, between the English and foreign Reformation, lay in this—that *we* retained, and *they* lost, the sacramental system. The name, Priest, which they have consistently rejected, and we as consistently have preserved, is the token and seal of that system, and so of our distinctiveness.

It is evident, then, from what source there first arose in England any opposition to the Catholic doctrine of the Priesthood. Urgent and persevering were the endeavours of the Swiss Reformers to advance their views amongst us. The second Prayer-Book of Edward VI., compared with the first of that reign, indelibly marks their fatal influence for a time.[1] But even while other

[1] See, among other accounts of the times, Cardwell's Preface to the "Two Liturgies of Edward VI. compared," in which many interesting details, bearing expressly on the point, are brought together by a philosophical and accomplished scholar. Cardwell proves that it was Calvinism, the extreme anti-Church element of the Reformation, not Lutheranism, that marred (may it not be added, without imputing evil motives to the agents, helped to desecrate?) the natural progress of the Reformation in England.

truths were temporarily suppressed during these sore and critical struggles, the name and idea of Priest remained undisturbed. The name was preserved in the second Prayer-Book of Edward VI., when Church principles were at their lowest ebb, and Calvinism had obtained its greatest influence, equally as in the first, or in the third, that of the reign of Queen Elizabeth, which we now use.

Calvinism has failed to rob us of our legitimate heritage; but it has succeeded in largely leavening the popular mind, so as to make in great measure practically inoperative, or a matter of reproach, much of what it could not remove. Under the specious guise of honouring the religion of the heart, and the soul's secret communings with GOD, it has really dwarfed and impoverished the spiritual life of multitudes, by destroying the popular faith in the Priesthood and in sacraments; thus loosening the hold of those "joints and bands" by which the Church, "having nourishment ministered, and knit together, increaseth with the increase of GOD." The popular arguments now prevailing, with the semblance (for, as hereafter will be shown, it is no more than the semblance) of Scriptural authority, are precisely those which are found in the Helvetic Confession of faith, as the self-asserted plea of Presbyterianism. It is but a consistent succession of doctrine, when the Presbyterian Vitringa gives the weight of his extensive learning to sustain what Calvin originated.[1]

---

[1] It is a remarkable instance of the uniformity of the laws which regulate the human mind, that in the struggles which attended the Reformation of the Church in Russia, two communities were formed, resembling the Lutherans and the Calvinists in the very point which we

are now considering. They both separated from the orthodox communion in 1656. The greater division, having among them some Priests, preserved the idea and functions of the Priesthood, with creeds and ritual. The other division, having neither Priest nor deacon, instituted a new and irregular ministry, to whom no semblance of a sacerdotal character belonged. The followers of the one are called "Popófchins," i.e., sectaries having priests; the others, "Bez-popófchins," i.e., sectaries having no priesthood.

But here the resemblance ceases. The Popófchins, unlike the Lutherans, never conceived the possibility of their Priests ordaining their successors; yet Priests, they said, must be had, for without Priests there could be no sacraments. An extraordinary course was adopted, and has been continued to this present day. Whosoever of the Priests of the old Church is known to be discontented, or in danger of punishment, or deprived, they offer him a stipend if he will abandon his Church and join them, and be their Priest. If he consent, the Priests that are among them first put him to penance, and give him absolution, and then use his ministrations; and thus the service of their altars has been sustained uninterruptedly to this present day. The other body of sectaries, which had no Priests, have never since sought them. But, unlike the Calvinists, they never admitted the idea that, by an inward act of their own mind, they could make a sacrament; for a sacrament, they felt, needed a Priest. The expedient to which they had recourse was this: they have persuaded themselves that there are preserved among them holy mysteries,—i.e., consecrated bread, moistened from the chalice and dried, as is usual for the communion of the sick. The blessed Sacrament thus preserved, they take and mix perpetually with fresh dough and fresh wine, so as to multiply to any extent, as they need, the elements, thus, as they suppose, already consecrated. (Twenty-first Dissertation on subjects relating to the Orthodox Communion. By the Rev. William Palmer.)

CHAPTER V.

THE COMMISSION AND FUNCTIONS OF THE PRIESTHOOD IN THE CHURCH OF ENGLAND.

IT has been shown how the term, Priest, was employed in the translation of our Prayer Book, in the face of a powerful opposing influence, which denounced the term as un-Scriptural and superstitious, and was thus clothed with the full authority of the Church. Nothing, however, has as yet been said of the distinctive ministry which this term designates. In order to ascertain this, the commission of the Priest, and the rules of our Service books determining his functions, are to be considered.

The Priest's commission runs in those awful words, which, being but an enlargement of the original words of institution, seem to prolong the accents of His Voice, Who breathed the grace of ordination on His Apostles. "Receive the HOLY GHOST for the Office and Work of a Priest in the Church of GOD, now committed unto thee by the Imposition of our hands. Whose sins thou dost forgive, they are forgiven; and whose sins thou dost retain, they are retained. And be thou a faithful Dispenser of the Word of GOD, and of His holy Sacraments; In the Name of the FATHER, and of the SON, and of the HOLY GHOST. Amen."

Three ideas are embodied in the terms of this commission; (1), the power of absolution; (2), authority to teach; and (3), the administration of the Sacraments. Though these distinctive functions are expressed only in the commission given to the second order of the ministry, yet they are not limited to that order; for a measure of the grace of the Priesthood extends to the Diaconate. The grace of the Priesthood in its fulness resides in the Bishop alone, and in passing through his hands, it is restrained or enlarged according to certain known laws of the Church. One sacramental rite, Confirmation, has always been reserved to the Bishop. On the other hand, the administration of Baptism, and authority to teach with the Bishop's licence, are committed to Deacons.[1] The Deacon so far acts as a Priest; the only difference being, that the authority to teach is inherent in the second order by virtue of the office, and is not dependent on licence from the Bishop.

The celebration of the Holy Eucharist, absolution, and the authority to bless in the Name of GOD, which is included under the administration of Sacraments, have never been extended beyond the second order. These three functions are the characteristic attributes of that order, or of the Priest properly so called, and to

---

[1] The rule of the Western Church extended the power of administering Holy Baptism to laymen in cases of extreme necessity. The English Church for many years after the Reformation continued the custom, but to prevent possible irregularity, at the last revision of the Prayer Book, this permission was withdrawn, and our Church, though not disallowing the validity of lay baptism, yet requires by her rule that the Sacrament be administered by "a lawful minister," i.e., one ordained according to the laws of the Church.—See the Rubrics in the Office for private Baptism.

these alone, therefore, our attention may be confined. The nature of these ministries, and the rules under which they are exercised, are determined by the rubrics and offices of the Prayer Book.

And first, with regard to absolution. Before every communion the Priest is directed to offer to all whose consciences are burdened, or beset with scruples, the opportunity for private confession and absolution, which to such persons the Church recommends. "If there be any of you, who cannot quiet his own conscience, but requireth further comfort or counsel, let him come to me, or to some other discreet and learned minister of GOD's Word, and open his grief; that by the ministry of GOD's Holy Word he may receive the benefit of absolution," &c.[1] Again, in the service for the Visitation of the Sick, the Priest is directed even to "move" the sick person "to make a special confession of his sins, if

---

[1] A strange interpretation has been adopted by some persons of the meaning of "absolution" in the exhortation before Holy Communion; as though it were intended only that the Priest should give to one who has "opened his grief," an assurance of the mercy of GOD, by repeating the promises of Holy Scripture, and encouraging him to believe them. But why is a Priest necessary to do what any intelligent Christian might do equally well? This interpretation, moreover, cannot possibly satisfy the meaning of the expression, "*benefit* of absolution." When we pray in the Post-Communion that we may receive "all the benefits of His Passion," does it mean merely that by seeing the broken Bread we may be assured of the truth of His Passion? The Prayer Book, like every other book, ought to be interpreted by itself, and if, in the Visitation of the Sick, it directs the Priest to give absolution, specifying the form in which it is to be given, and meaning consequently not the mere assurance of divine mercy, but the *act of absolving from sin*, we must conclude that the same act is intended, and the same form is to be used, whenever private confession is made, if the penitent desire it, and the Priest judge it to be applicable.

he feel his conscience troubled with any weighty matter;" and then after confession " to absolve him, if he humbly and heartily desire it."

Absolution remits actual sin, as Baptism remits original sin in infants, and in adults both original and actual sin alike. It is the instrument of restoration and peace, as Baptism is of initiatory life and union with God. Absolution is the essential correlative of Baptism; for as the grace of Baptism may be forfeited by sin, there needs other means of grace to restore what is lost. To supply this need Absolution was ordained of God. It is the restorative and remedial, as Baptism is the regenerating, element in the sacramental system, and the blessed Eucharist the food and sustenance of previously existing life.

The form of words with which Absolution is to be given, after private confession, is expressly appointed by the Church, and closely corresponds with the terms of the priest's commission, on which the authority of the act is grounded. The words do not merely imply a promise, or declaration of God's mercy: nor are they an expression of power as properly belonging to the person who speaks. Actual forgiveness is imparted, but it is not the gift of the Priest. It is God Who forgives; but He forgives by His minister. The words of Absolution involve an act done, pardon really bestowed; but at the same time they show, that the Priest who conveys it, acts only as an instrument, in the name and authority of God, as Christ's commissioned representative. In the words used, therefore, reference is made to the commission which Christ gave, as the ground of the validity of the act, and to true repentance on the part of the recipient as the indispensable condition required by Him. "Our LORD JESUS CHRIST, Who hath left power to His Church to absolve all sinners who truly repent and turn unto Him, of His great mercy forgive thee thine offences; and by His authority committed unto me, I absolve thee from all thy sins, in the Name of the FATHER, the SON, and the HOLY GHOST. Amen."

Under the head of the ministry of Absolution is included, as a further charge, intimately connected with it, the special guidance of souls. Together with "the benefit of Absolution," the priest is directed to offer "ghostly counsel and advice," so that by this twofold ministry may be obtained "the quieting of the conscience, and avoiding of all scruple and doubtfulness."

The ministry of the Holy Eucharist, from its pre-eminent importance, requires a more detailed consideration. The specially sacerdotal part of this office commences with the offertory. The offerings of the people are made to GOD in acknowledgment of their dependence upon Him, and especially of the inestimable benefits of redemption. They consist of two parts; alms for the relief of CHRIST's poor, and bread and wine, which are to be set apart from all other use, to be made the Sacrament of the Body and Blood of CHRIST, and consumed by the worshippers. They are separately offered by the celebrant, who is "humbly to present" them before GOD, and place the sacred vessels containing the gifts for the Eucharist in order upon the altar. He presents them as one ordained of GOD to offer gifts and sacrifices for men, and as the representative of the flock of CHRIST, acting on their behalf. The oblations, which are to become the materials of a sacrifice, must first be offered;

for every sacrifice supposes a previous offering of the thing to be sacrificed. The prayer that follows expressly distinguishes between the "alms" for the poor, and the "oblations," or gifts of bread and wine.[1] With these oblations, as yet unconsecrated, a solemn remembrance is made in prayer of the needs of the whole Church on earth, together with a commemoration of the dead who are at rest: thus fitly expressing the unity of the offerers with the whole mystical Body of CHRIST, while they offer the gifts in token that they, "being many, are one bread and one body; for we are all partakers of that one bread."

Three separate acts of ministry follow: (1) the consecration of the elements; (2) the oblation of the consecrated elements; (3) the administration.

(1.) Consecration does not here mean setting apart, or dedicating to GOD: this has been already done. The gifts of bread and wine were dedicated and set apart when they were presented on the altar, and in prayer offered

[1] "And if there be a Communion, the Priest" is then also "to place upon the Table so much bread and wine as he shall think sufficient,"—"which rubric, being added to our own Liturgy at the same time with the insertion of the term, 'oblations' in the prayer following, (i.e., at the last review,) it is clearly evident, as Bishop Patrick has observed, that by that word are to be understood the elements of bread and wine, which the Priest is to offer solemnly to GOD, as an acknowledgment of His sovereignty over His creatures; and that from thenceforth they might become properly and peculiarly His. For in all the Jewish sacrifices, of which the people were partakers, the viands or materials of the Feast were first made GOD'S by a solemn oblation, and then afterwards eaten by the communicants, not as man's, but as GOD'S provision; Who, by thus entertaining them at His own Table, declared Himself reconciled and again in covenant with them."—Wheatley, Illustration of the Common Prayer.

to the Divine Majesty. The object now is to effect, through the power of the HOLY GHOST, that further end which our LORD effected at the first institution, viz., to connect "the inward, invisible grace," with "the outward and visible sign," and thus make the Sacrament. Every fresh act of consecration is commanded to be for the same end, and with the same intention, which characterised our LORD's own act when He "blessed," "gave thanks," and said, "This is My Body," "This is My Blood;" for He commanded us to do as He had done. The act is based on the belief that the inanimate creatures lying on the altar are capable, through GOD's power, of being changed from their natural state, and becoming, after some supernatural manner, yet without losing their own substance or properties, the veils and organs of a true, substantial Presence of the Body and Blood of CHRIST. How it can be that a real, substantial Presence of CHRIST is possible on our altars, while yet He abides in the natural substance of His Flesh and Blood at the Right Hand of His FATHER; or how bread and wine, remaining in their natural substances, become associated with a new and Divine Substance, is not given to us to know. Both are true. The elements are real bread and wine; and they are the Flesh and Blood of CHRIST truly, but in a mystery. All that we know is, that the Presence of the LORD in the Sacrament is not effected by His moving from one place to another, nor is It after such a manner as is proper to material substances; but spiritually,—i.e., after a manner proper to spiritual substances. We believe that His Body and His Blood are, through ineffable union with His Divinity, capable of being made present elsewhere than in

THE COMMISSION AND FUNCTIONS OF A PRIEST. 37

the heavens; and present not merely by virtue and effect, Himself being absent, but Himself present, and by reason of His Presence imparting that virtue and effect. Human sense recognizes the reality of the consecrated symbols. Divine faith pierces the veil, and recognizes within it the Real Presence of Him Who is invisible.

This is no explanation of the mystery; it *is* a mystery, and we cannot explain it. For we know nothing of the manner in which spiritual substances are present in any place; or how that mode of presence which is proper to spiritual substances can become the property of material substances; or how our Blessed LORD's sacred Body, being material, is, through union with His Divinity, capable of such a Presence on earth, as we believe. Of the change, therefore, which passes on the natural substances of bread and wine, or of the Presence of CHRIST under the forms of the sacred symbols on the altar, we can give no account or sensible proof. "We believe it, because the Truth has spoken it; because the shadows of the Law have passed away, and the Body is come, even the Body of CHRIST; and there are no more empty forms, and the HOLY GHOST abides with us, and is able to change nature into grace." The bread which we see, and hold, and eat, is the Figure of His Body, but of His Body present, not absent; for He tells us, "THIS *is* My Body;" and in simplicity of faith we believe the words, believing that He is able to effect what He says, "without doing any violence to the natural laws of material substances, or to the conclusions of the human understanding."

The whole order of the Institution implies that the elements acquire their new properties by GOD's act, through the instrumentality of the Priest by consecration, and not through the faith of the communicant at a subsequent part of the service, or by the effect of the whole service generally. For until the prayer of consecration the elements are simply bread and wine. In that portion of the consecration prayer, which commences, "Hear us, O Almighty GOD, we most humbly beseech Thee, and grant," &c., the Priest prays that receiving the bread and wine may be the same as receiving the Body and Blood of CHRIST; and by the repetition of the words of institution, "In the same night that He was betrayed He took bread," &c., our LORD's own act is renewed. Immediately afterwards the Sacrament is administered, and what is administered is not mere bread and wine, but as the Catechism declares, "the Body and Blood of CHRIST, which are verily and indeed *taken* and *received;*" and the Article more strongly still, "The Body of CHRIST is *given, taken*, and eaten." If the Body and Blood of CHRIST are "given, taken, and received," they must have been made present before the communicant approaches.

Thus two momentous facts are determined by the express teaching of the Church, witnessed by the Liturgy, the Catechism, and the Articles,—(1) that "the inward, invisible grace" of the Sacrament is attached to its "outward and visible form;" (2) that this change is effected through the act of consecration.

(2) The act of consecration is accompanied with the further act of oblation; for as there was a first oblation of the gifts, that they might be set apart to GOD's honour and use, so, after their change by consecration, there is a second oblation, known as the Great Oblation,

in order to represent before the FATHER the Death and Passion of His SON. Two distinct uses are commanded by Holy Scripture to be made of the consecrated elements. By them we are to "shew forth the LORD's Death till He come," and afterwards to receive them in Holy Communion. We make of them a Sacrifice, and then they become our Food. This Oblation is involved in the very nature of the institution; for our LORD first offered Himself in the Eucharist as a Victim, before He was "delivered into the hands of wicked men to be crucified and slain," and as He continues to offer Himself now in the heavens. The words He uttered express that offering of Himself at that time. For He said, "This is My Body, which is given[1] for you." So also with the cup,—" This cup is the New Testament in My Blood which is shed" (lit. as a libation, or drink-offering, poured forth) "for you." He first offered Himself to the FATHER *for* us, and then gave Himself *to* us as our

---

[1] διδόμενον, S. Luke; κλώμενον, S. Paul; ἐκχυνόμενον, S. Matt., S. Mark, S. Luke,—the present tense, equivalent to *is being*. See Wordsworth on S. Matt. and S. Paul, in loc.

Some seeking to remove a supposed difficulty have considered this tense as a present-future, equivalent to *about to be* . . . They have limited their idea of the Oblation to the Crucifixion, and thought that our LORD could therefore have spoken at the time of the Supper only of a future Offering.

The truer view is, that our LORD's offering of Himself commenced with His first coming, His Life being a perpetual Sacrifice; that in the Eucharist, when He instituted It, He first sealed this Offering of Himself in a mystery directly applying Its benefits; that on the Cross He consummated the Offering in Death which constituted Its meritorious efficacy and power to redeem; that in Heaven He continues the Offering of Himself to perpetuate its benefits, even as His Priests on earth continue to plead the Same Offering on the altars of the Church.

The tense which our LORD employs embraces all time, because the one Offering is ever before GOD as an everlasting Present.

Food. And since He commanded us to do as He had done, therefore this same Oblation is to be perpetually renewed after the same manner.

The view taken of the Sacrifice in the Eucharist follows upon the view taken of the effects of consecration. We believe not the bread and wine to be mere figures, and thus reduce the Blessed Sacrament to a Jewish rite; nor do we believe that CHRIST is present after the natural laws of material substances, so that He can be sacrificed again, as He was sacrificed on the Cross. But we believe His Body and His Blood to be really present, under the forms of the consecrated symbols; and therefore, when we offer them, we offer His Body and His Blood really, though in a Sacrament or mystery. It is not a repetition of the sacrifice of the Cross,—thus He has been offered "once for all;" but it is a repetition of His offering Himself in the first celebration of the mystery, and a representation[1] of His continual offering of Himself now in heaven, and by it we point to and plead before the FATHER the one perfected Sacrifice of the Cross, through the merits of which alone we can approach and make our offering. This is the "unbloody Sacrifice" of the Church; "unbloody," because the Body and Blood of CHRIST are present after spiritual, not material, laws of being; and yet true and real, because the material things which are offered, are become true symbols and organs of the Real Presence of the One atoning Victim.

This Oblation, moreover, is made for the same ends and purposes for which our LORD offered Himself. And

---

[1] This term is used in its *proper* sense; i.e., *rem præsentem facere*, not *repræsentare*.

as He offered Himself for all for whom He was about to die,—not for the living only, but for those also who had gone before, and those who were to come afterwards,—so our Sacrifice is offered, not merely for those present, or those only who are alive on earth, but for those also who have "died in faith," and for the children yet unborn; for the whole body, or for individual members of the body whom we would specially remember before GOD. This Oblation is made in act and by implication only, at this part of the celebration; but in the prayer, known among ritualists as "the prayer of oblation,"—which, in the first Prayer Book of Edward VI., as in the ancient service-books, formed part of the prayer of consecration, but now follows the administration, and forms part of the Post-communion office,—the Oblation is expressed in words; "O LORD, Heavenly FATHER, we, Thy humble servants, entirely desire Thy Fatherly goodness, mercifully to accept *this our sacrifice of praise and thanksgiving*,"—the ordinary phrase used by the Fathers to denote the sacramental Offering of the Body and Blood of CHRIST.[1]

Then also is expressed the object and desire with

[1] Mede thus sums up the various synonymous terms used by the Fathers:—"The names by which the ancient Church called this service are—Oblation, Sacrifice, Eucharist, Sacrifice of Thanksgiving, Sacrifice of Praise, Reasonable and Unbloody Sacrifice, Sacrifice of our Mediator, Sacrifice of the Altar, Sacrifice of our Ransom, Sacrifice of the Body and the Blood of CHRIST." (Christian Sacrifice, lib. ii. c. iv.) As under the Old Covenant the term sacrifice was used in a twofold sense, denoting either that which was specially offered, or the whole service and ceremonies which accompanied the offering; so, in its application to the Holy Eucharist, it meant either the Sacramental Oblation itself, or the entire Liturgy, though primarily the former.

which the Oblation is made,—" most humbly beseeching Thee to grant that, by the merits and death of Thy SON JESUS CHRIST, and through faith in His Blood, we, and all Thy whole Church, may obtain remission of our sins, and all other benefits of His Passion." In making our first oblation of bread and wine, the petition was confined to the " whole state of CHRIST'S Church militant here on earth;" only at the close of the prayer commemorating the dead, blessing GOD for their memories, and stirring up ourselves to imitate their examples. But now, having the profound consciousness of our LORD'S Presence before us, and pleading the full merits of His Sacrifice, mystically represented before the FATHER, our hearts are enlarged, so as to comprehend all the needs and the longings of the entire communion of His elect; and we pray that both the departed, now at rest, their struggles over, may, whereinsoever they are wanting, be perfected, and those present, and all now on earth passing along their course of trial, may be fulfilled with grace. The expressions employed are of the widest possible extent,—"*all Thy whole* Church" being the subject of the prayer; and " the remission of sins, and *all other benefits* of the Passion,"—those which are necessary for the consummation of the bliss of the departed, as well as for the perfect cleansing of the living, —its object. The propitiatory virtue of the Holy Eucharist consists in this,—that it is the appointed means of pleading and applying the efficacy of the Cross; not as making a fresh atonement, or adding anything to the efficacy of that Sacrifice which is "finished," but as a means bringing out into act and effect its all-availing power, and thus communicating its benefits.

(3.) The administration of the Holy Communion follows. The Priest says to each communicant, "The Body (or the Blood) of our LORD JESUS CHRIST, Which was given (or shed) for thee," &c. And these words can bear no other interpretation than that the elements have been changed, and become the symbols of the Real Presence, before they are given; the communicant responding with an act of faith, that their full virtue may be received. The Communion is the consummation of the Sacrifice; for, as in the types of the Old Covenant, the sacrifice was partaken of and consumed, in token that it had been accepted, and the worshipper reconciled to GOD, so the same effect is produced in the Holy Eucharist, only with this difference, that there is now received, not the mere shadow, but "the very image of those things," which had been foreshadowed, even the Flesh and Blood taken of the Virgin's womb, which, having been transformed through union with GOD, and once for all sacrificed, is now perpetually presented before the FATHER, here veiled in mystery, openly in heaven, and given to us to become our own, a source of pure, supernatural, and endless life, so that we may be made, not only of one Spirit with CHRIST, but "bone of His Bone, and flesh of His Flesh."

After Communion, the offering of the Sacrifice of CHRIST is followed by the offering up of "ourselves, our souls and bodies;" that as the SON of GOD in our body made the willing offering of Himself for us, so we, through His mighty transforming power, being united to Him, should offer up ourselves "a reasonable, holy, and lively sacrifice unto" GOD; that through Him now dwelling in us, and we in Him, the "offering up of the

Church may be acceptable," and our union of nature and of will with CHRIST complete.

The benediction closes this mystical and life-giving act of our religion, in which, through the ministry of a Priest, and, according to the universal law of the Church, of a Priest alone, by authority transmitted through the Apostles from CHRIST Himself, the Real Presence, Oblation, and participation of His very Body and Blood, for the remission of sins, and all other benefits of His Passion, are continually renewed; and the Church, in return, offers itself to GOD in a blessed, mutual communion.

The third specific ministry of a priest is that of blessing in the Name of the Most Holy TRINITY. The act of blessing is one of the sacramental mysteries of the kingdom of GOD. It is connected with the act of sacrifice, or rather is a consequence of the same ministry; for to bless is solemnly to set apart and dedicate, by invoking the grace of GOD on what is thus dedicated to Him. Under former dispensations, special acts of blessing were generally preceded by sacrifice. In the ordinary daily service of the temple, "the people waited without" till the Priest, after offering the sacrifice, came forth to bless them. Throughout our public services, wherever a benediction is given, or implied, a Priest is, by express rubric, appointed to minister.[1] Although such acts as

---

[1] In the Marriage service, the first blessing is to be given by the "minister;" but this term is frequently used as synonymous with Priest. In the first rubric in the Marriage service, as well as in giving the final blessing, the priest is expressly mentioned as the person officiating. In the Confirmation service, the blessing is given by the Bishop, who is a priest,

the solemnisation of marriage, or the burial of the dead, (which service implies the last blessing of the Church on the departed members of CHRIST's Body,) are sometimes performed by deacons, yet this is an irregularity, and has arisen only in consequence of the too great pressure of constraining duties on Priests in large parishes. In our Marriage and Burial services alike the rubrics throughout speak of the Priest, implying that he is present and officiating.

That the ministry of blessing is connected with the ministry of sacrifice, appears from the fact, that the fullest and most solemn Christian blessing, "The peace of GOD, which passeth all understanding, &c.," is directed to be given only at the close of the Eucharistic Sacrifice; not as though it may not fitly be given at other times, but as being then most peculiarly appropriate—the highest act of Christian benediction flowing forth from the highest act of Christian sacrifice.

Taking, then, the terms of the commission, interpreted and illustrated by the rules and services of the Prayer-Book, as a guide to the meaning of the word,

and more than a priest. In the Churching of women, which includes an offering, and in the Burial service, the rubrics mention the priest throughout as the person intended to officiate.

The distinctive sense of 'minister' appears in the 32nd Canon, "That none be made deacon and minister both in one day." This title is explained in the body of the Canon to mean, that "there may ever be some time of trial of their behaviour in the office of deacon, before they be admitted to the order of priesthood." As the greater contains the less, so minister, a more general term than priest, is often employed in rubrics to denote offices which may be also performed by deacons, as, e.g., in reciting prayers.

Priest, and the distinctive character of his ministry, we obtain the following description:—A Priest is one who teaches the Word of GOD with authority; receives confessions, absolves and guides souls; consecrates the symbols of the Passion; offers the commemorative Sacrifice; dispenses the Sacred Food of the Sacrifice, even the blessed Body and Blood of the LORD; blesses in the Name of the Most Holy TRINITY; and administers all offices in which either offerings or special intercessions are made to GOD, or Divine benedictions are bestowed.[1]

[1] The following extracts from commentators and devotional writers on the English Communion Office will serve to confirm the explanations given in the text. The extracts are confined to the doctrine of the Sacrifice, and propitiatory efficacy of the Holy Eucharist:—

Bishop Overall. Notes on the Common Prayer in Nicholls' Commentary. "If we compare the Eucharist with CHRIST's Sacrifice made once upon the Cross, as concerning the effect of it, we say that *that* was a *sufficient* Sacrifice; but withal that *it* is a true, real, and *efficient* Sacrifice, and *both* of them propitiatory for the sins of the whole world. And therefore, in the oblation following," (the "prayer of oblation" is alluded to,) "we pray that it may prevail so with GOD, as that we and all the whole Church of CHRIST, (which consists of more than those that are upon the earth,) may receive the benefit of it. Neither do we call this Sacrifice of the Eucharist an *efficient* sacrifice, as if that upon the Cross wanted efficacy; but because the force and virtue of that Sacrifice would not be profitable unto us, unless it were applied and brought into effect by this Eucharistical Sacrifice, and other the holy Sacraments and means appointed by GOD for that end: but we call it propitiatory both this and that, because they have both force and virtue in them to appease GOD's wrath against this sinful world. Therefore this is no new Sacrifice, but the same which was once offered, and which is every day offered to GOD by CHRIST in heaven, and continueth here still on earth by a mystical representation of it in the Eucharist; and the Church intends not to have any new propitiation, or new remission of sins obtained, but to make that effectual, and in act applied unto us, which was once obtained by the Sacrifice of CHRIST upon the Cross. Neither is the Sacrifice of the Cross, as it was once offered up there, *modo cruento,* so much regarded in the Eucharist, though it bo commemorated, as regard is had to the perpetual and daily offering of it by CHRIST now in heaven in His everlasting Priesthood; and thereupon was, and should be still, the *juge Sacrificium* observed here on earth as it is in heaven, the reason which the ancient Fathers had for their daily sacrifice."

Bishop Cosin. Notes on the Common Prayer: on the "Prayer of Oblation." "In the celebration of the Sacrament of the Eucharist, GOD'S SON and His SON'S Death (which is the most true Sacrifice) is represented by us to GOD the FATHER, and by the same representation, commemoration, and attestation is offered; and that (as will appear from what will be afterwards said) for the living and for the dead, i.e., for the whole Church: for as CHRIST Himself, now He is in heaven, does appear in the Presence of GOD for us, making intercession for us, and does present and offer Himself and His Death to GOD; so also the Church upon earth, which is His Body, when it beseeches GOD for His sake and His Death, does also represent and offer Him and His Death, and consequently that Sacrifice which was performed on the Cross. No one is so blind as not to see the difference between a 'proper offering,' which was once performed by His Death on the Cross, and between an 'improper offering,' which is now made either in heaven by that His appearance on our behalf, or here on earth by prayer and representation, or attestation, or commemoration; there being only the same common name for these, but a very wide difference in the things themselves. . . . .

"'That we and all Thy whole Church may obtain remission of our sins, and all other benefits of His Passion:' where by all 'the whole Church' is to be understood, as well those who have been heretofore, and those who shall be hereafter, as those that are now the present members of it. And hereupon my Lord of Winchester, Bishop Andrewes, propounded his answer to Cardinal Perron, when he said, 'We have and offer this Sacrifice both for the living and the dead; as well for them that are absent, as those that be present,' or words to this purpose, for I have not the book now by me."

Bishop Sparrow. Rationale upon the Book of Common Prayer. "Now that no man take offence at the word 'altar,' let him know that anciently both these names, 'altar,' or 'holy table,' were used for the same things, though most frequently the Fathers and Councils use the word 'altar.' And both are fit names for that holy thing: for the Holy Eucharist, being considered as a Sacrifice, in the representation of the breaking of the bread and pouring forth the cup, doing that to the holy symbols which was done to CHRIST'S Body and Blood, and so showing forth and commemorating the LORD'S Death, and offering upon it the same Sacrifice that was offered upon the Cross, or rather the commemoration of that Sacrifice, (S. Chrysostom in Heb. x. 9,) it may fitly be called an 'altar;' which again is as fitly called an 'holy table,' the Eucharist being considered as a Sacrament, which is nothing also but a distribution and application of the Sacrifice to the several receivers."

Bishop Taylor. Worthy Communicant, ch. i. sect. 4. "Now what CHRIST does in heaven, He hath commanded us to do on earth,—that is, to represent His Death, to commemorate His Sacrifice, by humble prayer and thankful record; and by faithful manifestation and joyful Eucharist, to lay it before the eyes of our Heavenly FATHER, so ministering in His Priesthood, and doing according to His commandment and example: the Church being the image of heaven; the priest the minister of CHRIST; the holy table being a copy of the celestial altar; and the Eternal Sacrifice of 'the Lamb slain from the beginning of the world' being always the same. It bleeds no more after the finishing of it on the Cross; but it is wonderfully represented in heaven, and graciously represented here; by CHRIST's action there, by His commandment here. And the event of it is plainly this,—that as CHRIST, in virtue of His Sacrifice on the Cross, intercedes for us with His FATHER, so does the minister of CHRIST's Priesthood here; that the virtue of the Eternal Sacrifice may be salutary and effectual to all the needs of the Church, both for things temporal and eternal. And therefore it was not without great mystery and clear signification that our Blessed LORD was pleased to command the representation of His Death and Sacrifice on the Cross should be made by breaking bread and effusion of wine."

Dean Comber. Companion to the Altar. "When can we more effectually intercede with GOD for the whole Church, than when we represent and show forth that most meritorious Passion on earth, by the virtue whereof our great High Priest did once redeem, and doth ever plead for His whole Church even now that He is in heaven? This Sacrament, therefore, hath been accounted the 'great intercession;' and, accordingly, all the ancient Liturgies did use such universal intercessions and supplications while this mystery was in hand; and in the time of S. Cyril there was a prayer used, exactly agreeing with this of our Church. S. Chrysostom also saith, that the priest, standing at the altar, did 'offer prayers and praises for all the world, for those that are absent and those that are present, for those that were before us, and those that shall be after us, while that Sacrifice is set forth.'"

Nelson. Great Duty of Frequenting the Christian Sacrifice. "When our SAVIOUR JESUS CHRIST celebrated the Jewish Sacrifice of the Passover, with His disciples, a little before His sufferings, He substituted the Sacrament of His Body and Blood as the true Christian Sacrifice, in the room of the Passover; and ordained it as a rite to invocate His FATHER by, instead of the manifold and bloody sacrifices of the Law, and to be a means of supplication and address to GOD in the New Testament, as they were in the Old. . . . We thereby represent to GOD the FATHER the Passion of His SON, to the end that He may, for His sake, according to the tenour of His covenant with Him, be favourable and propitious to us miserable sinners; that as CHRIST intercedes continually for us in heaven, by presenting His death and satisfaction, so the Church on earth, in like manner, may approach the Throne of Grace, by representing CHRIST unto His FATHER in these holy mysteries of His Death and Passion."

Sherlock. Practical Discourse on Religious Assemblies. "Now for this end was the LORD'S Supper instituted to be 'a remembrance' of CHRIST, or of the Sacrifice of the Cross, to 'show forth the LORD'S Death till He come,' which, as it respects GOD, is to put Him in remembrance of CHRIST'S death, and to plead the virtue and merit of it for our pardon and acceptance. It is a visible prayer to GOD to remember the sufferings of His SON, and to be propitious to His Church, His Body, and every member of it, which He has purchased with His own Blood. And for this reason the LORD'S Supper was called a commemorative Sacrifice, because we therein offer up to GOD the remembrance of CHRIST'S Sacrifice; and therefore, in the ancient Church, the altar, or the place where they consecrated the elements, was the place also where they offered up their prayers, to signify that they offered up their prayers only in virtue of the Sacrifice of CHRIST, and that the very remembrance of this Sacrifice in the LORD'S Supper, by virtue of its institution, did render their prayers prevalent and acceptable to GOD; and, therefore, in the very first account we have of the exercise of Christian worship, we find 'breaking of bread and prayers' joined together. The efficacy of our prayers depends on the merit of CHRIST'S Sacrifice; and the way CHRIST hath appointed to give our prayers an interest in His Sacrifice, is to offer them in the Holy Supper, with the sacramental remembrance of His Death and Passion."

Bishop Wilson. Sacra Privata: LORD'S Supper. A Prayer for

Priests before the Service begins: "May it please Thee, O GOD, Who hast called us to this ministry, to make us worthy to offer unto Thee this Sacrifice for our sins, and for the sins of Thy people."

Prayer to be used immediately after the Consecration: "May I atone Thee, O GOD, by offering to Thee the pure and unbloody Sacrifice which Thou hast ordained by JESUS CHRIST."

Holy Bible, with Notes—On S. Matt. xxvi. 28: 'Which is shed,'— "i. e., He then, at that instant, gave His Body and Blood a Sacrifice for the sins of the world. He then offered, as a Priest, Himself, under the symbols of bread and wine: and this is the Sacrifice which His Priests do still offer. And let it be observed, that JESUS CHRIST did this before He was apprehended, when He was at His own disposal; it was then that He offered Himself a Sacrifice to GOD."

Johnson. Primitive Communicant. "Praise the LORD, O my soul, all the days of thy life, for such a Priest (our LORD JESUS CHRIST), and for the oblation of His Body and Blood, which He commanded for ever to be continued in remembrance of Him; for the mysterious Bread given for the life of the world, for the Cup poured out for the remission of the sins of men. . . . Praise the LORD, O my soul, for this High Priest, according to the order of Melchisedek, and for this pure oblation of bread and wine, by which we serve all the ends, and obtain all, and more than all the benefits procured by the manifold sacrifices under and before the Law: of that bread and wine in the offering whereof CHRIST consigned Himself to the Cross, there to suffer death, and make a full satisfaction for the sins of all who should, with true, penitent hearts, apply themselves to Thee, through His all-sufficient Death and Sacrifice."

Wheatley. Illustration of the Common Prayer. On the Prayer of Consecration: "And this (the repetition of the words of institution) is certainly a very essential part of the service. For during the repetition of these words, the priest performs to GOD the representative Sacrifice of the Death and Passion of His SON. By taking the bread into his hand and breaking it, he makes a memorial to Him of our SAVIOUR'S Body broken upon the Cross; and by exhibiting the wine, he reminds Him of His Blood then shed for the sins of the world; and by laying his hand upon each of them at the same time that he repeats those words, 'Take, eat, this is My Body,' &c., and 'Drink ye all of this,' &c., he signifies and acknowledges that this commemoration of CHRIST'S Sacrifice, so made to GOD, is a means instituted by CHRIST Himself to convey to the communicants the benefits of His Death and Passion . . . For the Holy Eucharist was, from the very first institution, esteemed and received as a proper Sacrifice, and solemnly offered to GOD upon the altar, before it was received and partaken of by the communicants."

See the 81st number of the Tracts for the Times; to which is subjoined a complete catena of the principal English theologians since the Reformation, who have written in support of the doctrine of the Eucharistic Sacrifice, from which the few extracts above given have been selected.

It is to be observed, as a striking circumstance, in harmony with this doctrine, that the term, sacrifice, does not occur in the prayers of any Office of the English Prayer Book except that of the Holy Eucharist.

CHAPTER VI.

TESTIMONY OF THE POST-APOSTOLIC CHURCH, OR THE PERIOD SUBSEQUENT TO THE FIRST CENTURY OF CHRISTIANITY.

IF any doubt remain whether the Church of England considers her ministry to be clothed with a true sacerdotal character, its solution must be sought according to the principles of the Reformation, in the records of Holy Scripture and of the early undivided Church. And although, after the facts adduced, there can be no reasonable doubt upon the question, yet as the Church of England is not an ultimate authority, but only an organ or channel of the teaching of the Catholic Church and the Word of GOD, it is requisite for the full confirmation of the truth, to view the subject in the light of these higher authorities.

A distinction is to be made, for reasons which will subsequently be explained, between the evidence to be derived from the Apostolic period, or first century of Christianity, and that of succeeding ages. For the present our inquiry is confined to the latter period.

In order to obtain a full view of the mind of the Church, three points need to be considered, (1.) the names by which the Christian ministry and its functions were denoted; (2.) the principles of the chief public service celebrated; and (3.) the primitive doctrine of the propitiatory efficacy of the Holy Eucharist.

(1.) The question of names is of considerable importance, when we bear in mind that the Church was free to choose either the New Testament names for the ministry, to which as yet no sacerdotal meaning had been attached in the usage of mankind, or the ancient names, to which the world had been long accustomed, as denoting such a character. And as we believe that the Church was guided in these questions of essential truth by the HOLY SPIRIT, it must follow that the choice made was the fittest to represent the idea which was to be permanently inwrought into the Christian mind. As to the usage of the period to which our present inquiry is confined, there can be no surer authority than that of Vitringa himself. His extensive learning, directed assiduously to this very subject, and his zeal as a partizan, make his testimony to be peculiarly conclusive. In the "Prolegomena" (cap. 2) already referred to, he states the result of his researches in the following words:

"That Tertullian, in the beginning of the third century, calls the Bishop, Chief Priest (summus Sacerdos); that before his time, in the second century, Irenæus calls the gifts made at the holy Eucharist, oblations (oblata), and when consecrated by the prayer of the Bishop, a sacrifice (sacrificium); and that in Justin Martyr, a still more ancient writer, the gifts are called offerings (προσφοραί),—are facts so certainly known to the learned, that it is needless to speak of them at greater length. In the subsequent writings of the Fathers, the terms, Priesthood, Priest, Levites, altars, offertories, sacrifices, oblations, used in reference to the Church of the New Testament, are so obvious and frequent, that it can escape no one who has even cursorily examined their writings. In Eusebius, moreover, and the rest of the ecclesiastical historians, and the Canons of Councils, such frequent mention occurs of these phrases, that it is evident they must have struck deep root (altas egisse radices) into the minds of men in those ages." One passage he moreover quotes from S. Jerome, who in his famous letter to Evagrius, speaks of "the Apostolical tradition, that what Aaron and his sons and the Levites were in the Temple, that our Bishops, Priests, and Deacons claim to be in the Church." It would be needless to multiply proof on such a point.

It has been objected, however, that the ancient Fathers introduced the terms in question, in consequence of their prepossessions in favour of the sacerdotal system, to which before their conversion to Christianity they had been accustomed; and that, being men of intellect and power, they succeeded in leavening the mind of the Church with an idea which was but a perversion of the Scriptural and primitive view of the ministry. To judge of the probability of such a supposition, it must be borne in mind that, independently of man's natural tendency, in the case of conversion from one system to another, to take an extreme line in opposition to that which they have forsaken, the extant writings of these very men contain the strongest possible appeals against the heathen ceremonial; that, moreover, they ardently laboured by word and deed to destroy any reverence for the system of idolatry; and that they were subjected to frequent persecutions at the hands of the heathen. It seems inconceivable that sincere men, under such circumstances, should have agreed together (for their unanimity in the use of these terms is the very point which Vitringa notes as so remarkable) to borrow from a system thus reprobated, and thus still dangerous and personally hostile, terms which could only have been a perpetual snare to their disciples, perplexing and hindering the whole course of their teaching. The other and more reasonable explanation of the fact is, that there is a real principle, on which both heathens and Christians were agreed,—the principle of a sacerdotal system, of which the heathen was a perverted image, and which was to be realized according to the Divine mind only in Christianity.

Moreover, the consequences of such a supposition must be borne in mind. If those primitive Fathers were led astray on such a vital point, Satan having so far prevailed as to introduce heathen notions into the Church at the very time when the Catholic creeds were being formed, and in a matter which affected the inner life and entire system of the Church's devotion, and the very means of communicating the benefits of CHRIST's Incarnation and Death, how could we, under such circumstances, appeal to the Body of which these men are the recognized exponents and witnesses, as "the pillar and ground of the Truth," or feel any reliance in its testimony on any question whatever?

But however unscrupulous other communities of Christians who have systematically cast off all respect for Catholic testimony, might be, even under such a view of the case, it is impossible for an English Churchman to admit such a suspicion; for the Homily on the Blessed Sacrament (second part), speaking authoritatively, says: "But before all things, this we must be sure of especially, that this Supper be in such wise done and maintained, as our LORD and SAVIOUR did and commanded to be done, as the Holy Scripture used it, and as *the good Fathers of the primitive Church frequented it.*" And who are meant by "the good Fathers of the primitive Church," is explained in another authoritative record, which states them to be "the most notable Fathers who lived during the first five hundred years after CHRIST, such as Justin, Irenæus, Tertullian, Cyprian, Basil, Chrysostom, Jerome, Ambrose, Augustine,"[1] the very men who the most frequently and uniformly employed the terms in question.

It must be carefully borne in mind, in order to give full weight to this argument, that these terms thus used by the ancient Fathers, "offerings" (προσφοραί) and "sacrifices" (θυσίαι), are the very same which S. Paul in his Epistle to the Hebrews applies to our LORD's offering and sacrifice of Himself for the sins of the world.[2] The connection between His sacrifice and our sacrifice, and therefore the reality of a propitiation in the one as in the other, though the virtue of our Eucha-

---

[1] In the dispute between the advocates of the Church of England and those of the Church of Rome, in Westminster Abbey, in the reign of Queen Elizabeth, the former argued thus—"It is against the Word of GOD, and the custom of the primitive Church, to use a tongue unknown to the people. By these words (the Word) we mean only the written Word of GOD, or canonical Scripture; and by the custom of the primitive Church, we mean the one most generally used in the Church for the space of five hundred years after CHRIST, in which lived the most notable Fathers, as Justin," &c.

[2] Heb. ix. 14, 25, 26, 28; x. 10, 12, &c.

ristic offering rests wholly on the connexion, which by our Lord's ordinance exists between it and His one meritorious sacrifice, is in harmony with this use of the same terms as applied to both, and can scarcely be otherwise understood.

There is moreover a separate and peculiarly important line of evidence to be drawn from the ancient Liturgies. Even were it supposable that the Fathers, regardless of their tendency to mislead, used such terms as extreme expressions, or as mere metaphors, there is yet further and more momentous evidence to be drawn from the Church's Service Books.

Liturgies are acted creeds. As there are no human documents, in which words once introduced are less likely to be changed, so there are none in which the introduction of any term is made with more mature deliberation. There are four Liturgies which Mr. Palmer has shown to have been reduced to writing in the course, one of them in the earliest part, of the fourth century.[1] They are beyond comparison the most valuable witnesses we possess to the early Church's living faith and hope. These four Liturgies were used respectively at the central sees of the four great Patriarchates of Christendom and their subordinate branches, and through them pervaded the whole Catholic world.

"The first," to use Mr. Palmer's own words,[2] "is the great Oriental Liturgy, as it seems to have prevailed in all the Christian Churches from the Euphrates to the Hellespont, and from the Hellespont to the southern

---

[1] "Disputation on Primitive Liturgies," by the Rev. Wm. Palmer.
[2] Ibid.

extremity of Greece. The second was the Alexandrian, which from time immemorial has been the Liturgy of Egypt, Abyssinia, and the country extending along the Mediterranean Sea to the west. The third was the Roman, which prevailed throughout the whole of Italy, Sicily, and the civil diocese of Africa. The fourth was the Gallican, which was used throughout Gaul and Spain, and probably in the Exarchate of Ephesus until the fourth century." (Page 8.)

The remarkable phenomenon exhibited by these liturgies is, that in their general structure, their component parts, and even in their forms of expression, they correspond so closely one with another, as to leave no doubt of their having proceeded from one and the same source. Mr. Palmer observes: "The uniformity between these liturgies, as extant in the fourth and fifth centuries, is such as to bespeak a common origin. Their diversity is such as to prove the remoteness of the period at which they were originated. To what remote period can we refer, as exhibiting a perfect, general uniformity of liturgy, except to the Apostolic age?" Subsequently, he adds with regard to the Oriental liturgy: "Let us remember, also, that existing documents enable us to trace this liturgy to that period; and that in the time of Justin Martyr, to whose writings I allude, the Christian Church was only removed by one link from the Apostles themselves." (Sect. iii.)

Nor is this all; for there exists a fifth liturgy, of a still earlier date than either of the four already mentioned,—the Clementine. Its striking characteristic is, that it agrees with the four great liturgies in all points in which they agree with each other, as well as in their general structure. The supposition of ritualists is, that the Clementine liturgy was never actually used in any church, but that "it represented the general mode, prevalent throughout the Christian world during the first three centuries, of celebrating the Holy Eucharist;" and it seems highly probable, due allowance being made for changes that would naturally occur in the lapse of time, that this liturgy embodies the original form used by the Apostles themselves.[1]

Now in all these liturgies alike, the ancient sacerdotal terms in question are ordinarily used. In reading them we open upon a scene, which represents a priesthood of different degrees, with a complete ritual, ministering before GOD on behalf of the people, offering sacrifices, and communicating heavenly gifts and benedictions. It would be to anticipate a view of the subject which falls more naturally under our notice at a later stage of the inquiry, if we were here to follow out what has been suggested as to the probable source of these liturgies; but it is impossible to exaggerate the importance of the facts adduced, leading to the conclusion that the introduction of these disputed terms may

[1] It is the general opinion of ritualists, that the Church's Liturgy was not committed to writing for many generations, but that her priests were accustomed to recite the prayers from memory. The supposed reason was, to prevent the possibility of any records of the Holy Eucharist falling into the hands of persecutors. It is well known that the mode of celebrating the Holy Eucharist, was the special subject of inquiry by the heathen, and of special reserve on the part of the Church. They sought to cast the utmost mystery around the central life of their communion with the LORD. It is a remarkable circumstance, often noted, and tending to this conclusion, that while copies of the Holy Scriptures are known to have been seized in times of persecution, there is no record of any liturgy having met with the same fate.

be traced to Apostolic men, if not to the Apostles themselves.

(2.) These ancient liturgies fulfil a yet more important end, in support of the sacerdotal system, by exhibiting the original idea of the Church's service. For in order to ascertain the character of the ministry, its daily acts and living forms are of more importance than the mere names by which it was called. This further inquiry, moreover, is necessary, because the same theory which represents the Jewish elder as the prototype of the Christian minister, supposes also the Church's service to be the offspring, not of the temple, but of the synagogue.

The term liturgy, in the language of the Church, properly denotes, only the Office of the Holy Eucharist. The five great liturgies above alluded to, are confined to this service; and the prominent fact brought out by their history is, that the Eucharist was the primary and fundamental idea of Christian worship,—the centre around which all its other offices of prayer and praise were formed. It has been already stated, that the structure and component parts of these liturgies are, for the most part, alike in all; the only variation being, that some parts are missing in one which appear in another, and that the relative positions of the several parts vary. The following brief digest may give some idea of this system of devotion, into which the mind of Christendom was habitually casting itself in its communion with GOD. It will be readily seen, how the outline corresponds with our own Eucharistic Office.

One or more collects; lessons from Holy Scripture; a sermon, sometimes preceded by a hymn or anthem;

prayers for the catechumens, penitents, &c., who with a benediction were then dismissed; the creed; the offertory, with the oblations of bread and wine; thanksgivings and intercessions, with a commemoration of the dead in CHRIST, formed the earlier part of the service. Afterwards the more mystical portion of the liturgy commenced, and in all cases with the very same words, "Sursum corda," ("Lift up your hearts"); and then followed a thanksgiving closing with the Tersanctus; intercessory prayers; the consecration of the Elements, with the repetition of our LORD's words of institution; a second oblation of the now consecrated elements (this was not always expressed in words,—sometimes silently, and in act only); an invocation of the HOLY GHOST (this is not found in the Roman, nor in the Gallican Liturgies); intercessory prayers for the whole Church, the dead as well as the living; the LORD's Prayer; a benediction; the administration or communion; thanksgiving; the Gloria in Excelsis; and the final benediction.

It is evident how such a service, composed mainly of oblations mingled with intercessions and benedictions, the consecration, offering, and administration forming its central features, implies a ministry of a strictly sacerdotal character. It will hereafter be shown how impossible it is to trace up its complicated structure and deep mystery to the simple service of instruction and congregational prayer, which characterized the worship of the synagogue.

It would be wandering too far from our special object, to trace the history of the other services of the Church. It is only possible to point out the important additional evidence which is to be derived from Mr. Freeman's valuable researches into the "principles of Divine service."[1] The first volume of his work relates to the minor offices of daily prayer; and he has established the fact of their dependence upon the Eucharistic service, circling around it as satellites around their central orb. Mr. Freeman's volume must be studied to obtain a full knowledge of this most deeply interesting subject, the more interesting and valuable from his having treated it in a very earnest and devotional spirit. His conclusions, and their bearing upon the subject before us, may be judged of by the following brief extract:

"There is a natural impulse, in the case of any one who has recently participated in the Eucharist, to view prayer, praise, and other devotional actions in connection with that great rite, as modes of realising and carrying out the Eucharistic frame and position. The Church, by her daily offices, both recognises and formalises this rightful conception. Her ordinary public devotions are designed to be, to those who are in a position to use them as such, an expansion and carrying on of the Eucharistic functions and relations. To such the general act of public worship is but a further cementing of the Eucharistically imparted union with CHRIST, and with His Body, the Church : . . . a view, it may surely

[1] "The Principles of Divine Service. An Inquiry concerning the true manner of understanding and using the Order for Morning and Evening Prayer, and the Administration of the Holy Communion in the English Church. By the Rev. Philip Freeman, M.A."

In expressing his obligations to Mr. Freeman for his work, the writer would not be understood to subscribe to his position, that the daily celebration of the Eucharist was not the primitive practice, or that it is not good to restore it, where possible. The proofs given by Mr. Freeman seem to the writer, though he would express his dissent with great deference, to be inconclusive.

be said, which dignifies, while yet it duly subordinates, the act of ordinary worship." (Chap. xi. p. 204.)

The conclusion to which we are thus brought is this, that the Eucharist is the primary and essential idea of Christian worship, and that this service, containing a true sacrifice, involves the necessity of a sacerdotal ministry; and that thus, practically, every thought of communion with GOD, must have been associated, more or less, with those sacerdotal functions, through which it had been ordained that the very Bread of Life, of which "a man shall eat and not die," should be given.

(3.) But in order to realise the full force of the evidence derived from the principles of the Church's service, it is requisite to consider further the belief universally prevailing of the propitiatory virtue of the Holy Eucharist; for propitiation is popularly and justly held to be an essential attribute of priesthood.

It is to be observed, that the term "propitiatory" is used here, as before in reference to the English Eucharistic service, not as introducing a fresh ground of acceptance with GOD, but as a means or instrument, effectually applying the virtues of that perfect and sufficient Atonement which was "finished" on the Cross. The idea is grounded on the conviction, that what our LORD once did in offering Himself, needs, according to His own appointment, a sacramental system in the Church on earth, in order to perpetuate and apply its benefits.

The idea of propitiating GOD by sacrifices, which could have no virtue in themselves, irrespective of the Divine appointment, has universally prevailed amongst mankind. Sacrifices were originally ordained as the means of obtaining for the offerer, an interest in the "Lamb slain from the beginning of the world;" and so far as they effected this, they were propitiatory. This was the primary idea of worship. "He builded an altar unto the LORD, and called on the Name of the LORD," is the view that opens upon us in the earliest records of the Book of Genesis; and the complicated ceremonial of the law of Moses, was but an expansion of this primæval idea of sacrifice and prayer combined.

The ancient Church believed that the Sacrifice of CHRIST made no change in this system of intercourse between GOD and man. They believed that, as sacrifice was the means of propitiating GOD, because of its covenanted relation with the promised Atonement before it was accomplished, so, after it was accomplished, the same system was to be continued, to connect man with the Atonement which had been completed. They saw an identity of principle pervading the ancient prefigurative, and their own commemorative, systems; only with this momentous difference, exalting beyond measure the whole ministry and service of the Church, that what had been of old exhibited only in type or shadow, was now substantially, and in very truth conveyed to them,—the Divine Victim, Who had been but prefigured and anticipated of old, being now actually present and imparting Himself. Hence to their mind it followed, that if the typical sacrifices of the ancient world were propitiatory, because of their relation to CHRIST, still more must their Eucharistic service be thus availing.

But it is simpler, and to an English Churchman will be more conclusive, instead of making an independent inquiry into the doctrine of the early Church, to accept the conclusions of an English divine, who, in regard to this view of the subject, more fully than any other writer within our communion has recorded the results of his researches into the records of antiquity. Mede, in his "Christian Sacrifice," thus states his conclusions:

"They" (the ancient Fathers) "believed that our Blessed SAVIOUR ordained the Sacrament of His Body and Blood, as a rite to bless and invocate His FATHER by, instead of the manifold and bloody sacrifices of the Law.... The mystery of which rite they took to be this: that as CHRIST, by presenting His death and satisfaction to His FATHER, continually intercedes for us in heaven, so the Church semblably approaches the Throne of Grace, by representing CHRIST unto His FATHER in these holy mysteries of His Death and Passion." (Lib. ii. c. iv.) Among other authorities, Mede quotes, in proof of his conclusions, S. Cyril of Jerusalem, whom he represents as "a sure witness of that which was said and done in the celebration of the Eucharist, according to the use of his time." (A.D. 350.) "After that spiritual sacrifice," says S. Cyril, "that unbloody sacrifice, (i.e., after the thanksgiving and invocation of the HOLY GHOST upon the bread and wine, to make them the Body and Blood of CHRIST) was done, we do over that propitiatory sacrifice (ἐπὶ τῆς θυσίας ἐκείνης τοῦ ἱλασμοῦ) beseech GOD for the common peace of the Churches, for the good estate of the world, for their armies, &c., &c." Mede then proceeds: "And this is the manner of the Greek Liturgies, immediately upon the consecration of the gifts (viz., the bread and wine) to be the symbols of the Body and Blood of CHRIST, and the commemoration thereon of His Passion, Resurrection, and Ascension, to offer to the Divine Majesty, as it were over the LAMB of GOD then lying on the table, their supplications and prayers for the whole state of CHRIST's Church, and all sorts and degrees therein, together with all other their suits and requests; and that ever and anon interposing the word 'we offer' (προσφέρομεν) unto Thee for these and these; that is, we commemorate CHRIST in this mystical rite for them. This prayer, therefore, our author, Cyril, in the place before quoted, calls 'the prayer of the holy and most worthily dreaded Sacrifice (θυσίας) lying then upon the table,' and saith, 'it is a most powerful prayer, as that wherein we offer unto the Divine Majesty CHRIST, that was once slain for our sins, propitiating (ἐξιλεούμενοι) the merciful GOD for ourselves and others we pray for.'" (Lib. ii. c. 6.) Mede also quotes Eusebius, commenting thus on the 23rd Psalm, "Thou hast anointed my head with oil." "Herein," saith he, "are plainly signified the mystical unction and the venerable sacrifices of CHRIST's Table, whereby, propitiating GOD, (δι' ὧν καλλιέρουντες, litare, i.e. propitiare, placare numen,) we are taught to offer up all our life long, unto the LORD of all, unbloody and reasonable sacrifices, most acceptable to Him, by His most glorious High Priest, JESUS CHRIST." (Lib. ii. c. x.)

As an instance of the manner in which this great truth was brought out in the ancient liturgies, the following extract from the prayer of consecration in the Liturgy of S. Mark may be added: "Make, O LORD, this bread the Body, this cup the Blood of the New Testament of our LORD and GOD, that they may be to us who partake of them, for the gift of faith, for sobriety, and healing, and wisdom, and holiness, and renewal of soul, and body, and spirit; for the communion of the blessedness of eternal life and immortality; for the glorifying of Thy holy Name, for the remission of sins," &c., &c.; and then follow prayers for the Church at large, for all its members, whether on earth or departed hence.

To show further how the conviction of the propitiatory efficacy of the Holy Eucharist was associated even with minute details of life, Mede quotes a passage out of S. Augustine (Lib. xxii. De Civitate Dei): "But for the more full understanding," he says, "of the notion and practice of this age, take also a passage of S. Austin concerning one Hesperius, who, by the affliction of his cattle and servants, perceiving his country grange liable to some malignant power of evil spirits, entreated our Presbyters, in my absence, that some of them would go to the place, through the perseverance of whose prayers he hoped the evil spirits would be forced away. Accordingly, one of them went thither, and offered there the Sacrifice of CHRIST's Body, praying earnestly with all his might for the ceasing of the sore affliction; and it ceased forthwith through GOD's mercy." (Lib. ii. c. i.) Mede, in conclusion, adds the following brief testimony from Origen, (Hom. xiii. in Levit. c. xxiv.,) who, comparing the Eucharist to the showbread which every Sabbath was set for a memorial before the LORD, saith: "That," meaning the Eucharist, "is the only commemoration which renders GOD propitious to men." "Where note," says Mede, "both that this commemoration is made unto GOD as that of the showbread; and that the end thereof is to make Him propitious to men; according to that of S. Augustine, Lib. ix. c. xiii.,

'Those things which CHRIST exhibits in His Supper, faith having received them, interposeth them as a satisfaction and propitiation between our sins and GOD's wrath.'"

The ancient Church, therefore, evidently regarded the Holy Eucharist as the great means whereby on earth the Divine Presence of the LORD was continually brought near, and His Sacrifice represented and renewed in all its effects and purposes. There was in truth present to the mind of the faithful in those ages a living, intense conviction, fed by a childlike faith on the words of institution, that the symbols were one with the thing symbolized; the broken bread undistinguishable to faith from the crucified Body, through the mystical consecration; the commemorative sacrifice identified with the Sacrifice of the Cross, as one offering ever afresh presented before the FATHER; and with confidence of love, like that of the diseased woman, who clung to the garments as the instruments of healing virtue, not for their own sake, but because of His Form Whom that clothing enveloped, in Whom was Life, so the Church believed, that through the outward elements, which the LORD had vouchsafed to assume to Himself by the power of the HOLY GHOST to be the organs of His Living Presence, there flowed forth the fulness of His Incarnation, and all the benefits of His Passion. Thus adoring in the Blessed Sacrament His very Presence, and feeling the Fount of Life thence streaming into their souls, and all this effected by Divine power acting through a human ministration, how could they regard the line of the ministry, through which such grace was given, otherwise than as a priestly line?

CHAPTER VII.

TESTIMONY OF THE APOSTOLIC AGE, OR FIRST CENTURY OF CHRISTIANITY.

THE advocates of the Presbyter view of the ministry, unable to meet the overwhelming evidence against them in the ages, the records of which we have been considering, take refuge in the thought, that their theory was realized in the first century. They admit that the sacerdotal view had taken complete possession of the mind of the Church subsequently to the Apostolic age, but assert that it was a foreign principle superinduced upon primitive Christianity. They rest their argument upon the supposed fact that the term Presbyter, not Priest, was applied to the second order of the ministry throughout the Apostolic age, and refer to the writings of the Apostolic Fathers, S. Clement, S. Ignatius, &c., in proof of their assertion.

There is great difficulty in obtaining evidence as to the usage of the Church during the age in question, and this rendered it necessary to consider the testimony of the first century separately from that of succeeding ages. The difficulty arises from the paucity of materials: for if we except the "Shepherd of Hermas," a purely allegorical work, the extant writings of the Apostolic Fathers would not occupy more than an octavo volume of about thirty pages. If then it could be proved that the term, Priest, does not occur as the proper designation of the Christian minister in these records, no conclusion could be founded on the fact, for the amount of evidence is too small to prove anything as to the usage of the great body of Christians. The evidence moreover which has been adduced from the primitive liturgies touches upon this first century, and the probability shown to exist of the introduction of the sacerdotal terms into these liturgies during the Apostolic age, is to be set against any negative evidence drawn from the silence of the few extant writings referred to.

Moreover the real question is not whether the name, but whether the *idea* of Priesthood is found to exist in the extant writings of the Apostolic Fathers. The name may not have been as yet in common use, and yet the idea may have prevailed, as in patriarchal times the idea of Priesthood existed long before it obtained any peculiar or fixed appellation. It has been already shown that the Hebrew title of Priest, *Cohen*, does not appear in the Bible as applied to a single minister of the patriarchal line, and yet undoubtedly there existed a true line of priests from the beginning. Priesthood, moreover, is but one part of a complete system, and if other portions of the system are found to exist, it may be implied that the entire system was in being, and so the Priesthood also. It was a living system in the ages immediately succeeding the first century. And as in the case of a living creature, the discovery of any one organic member of the structure is a true ground-work for building up the entire form, and proves its existence at the time when that one member was in being, so a similar mode of reasoning may be employed in regard to the sacerdotal system of the Catholic Church.

The term, altar, may be taken as an instance. It is the term uniformly employed in connexion with the blessed Sacrament during the three first centuries. The word Table is only employed once in the extant writings of that period, and in the Apostolic Fathers not once. So likewise the terms 'offerings,' 'sacrifices,' are used equally by the Apostolic, as by the later Fathers. In the few epistles which remain of S. Ignatius, while the term altar is used occasionally, as a metaphor, to imply personal sacrifice, it occurs four times with express reference to the blessed Sacrament. One striking instance of the kind is to be found in the epistle to the Philadelphians (v.) : "Be zealous to frequent one Eucharist: for there is one Flesh of our LORD JESUS CHRIST, and one Cup for the union (ἕνωσιν) of His Blood, one altar, as there is one Bishop, with the Presbytery, and deacons my fellow labourers, that what ye do, ye may do according to GOD." Here we find combined in one view the altar, the Real Presence, the Communion of the Flesh and Blood, and the three orders of ministry; and all this declared to be "of GOD." The complicated and majestic structure of the Catholic liturgies was but a detailed exposition of the ideas embodied in these few striking words. A Priest was in later days the indispensable celebrant of the Church's liturgy; where is the difference between this later system and the principles exhibited in the writings of S. Ignatius?

There is moreover a passage in S. Clement's Epistle

to the Corinthians, which bears more directly on the question at issue.[1] He is exhorting the Corinthians to observe better order in their religious assemblies, especially in the celebration of the Eucharist, and he thus enforces his exhortations: "We ought therefore to do in order whatsoever the LORD commanded us to do at appointed seasons, and duly perform the oblations and sacred services (προσφορὰς καὶ λειτουργίας) : and where and by whom He wills them to be done, Himself hath determined. They who make their offerings at the appointed seasons, are accepted and blessed; for following the ordinances of the LORD, they do not err. For to the High Priest proper services have been assigned, and the priests have their proper place appointed, and on Levites proper ministrations have been laid. The layman has been bound by lay ordinances. Let each one of you, therefore, in his own order, offer the Eucharist (εὐχαριστείτω) to GOD, living in good conscience, without transgressing the appointed rule of his ministry."

Professor Jacobson, in his late edition of the Apostolic Fathers, quotes Wotton, expressing himself thus as to the application of the terms High Priest, Priest, and Levite, which occur in this passage, to the threefold Christian ministry:—"That the Jewish Church was the type of the Christian, and that the same orders were received among the Jews by the institution of GOD, which were admitted into the Church of CHRIST when the Mosaic dispensation was abolished, is the opinion of all ancient authors. Had the Jewish Church an High Priest, Priests, and Levites? The Christian also has

[1] Sec. 40.

Bishops, Presbyters, and Deacons." Wotton adduces, in confirmation of his views, the well-known passage of S. Jerome already referred to, and also a passage of S. Cyprian quoted in the following chapter, and then adds: "Although CHRIST alone is the High Priest of both covenants, yet the Bishop bears His office (ejus vices gerit) in the Church, not otherwise than the High Priest in the Temple."[1] Among modern scholars, Dr. Wordsworth, in his "Theophilus Anglicanus," adduces the passage as direct evidence of the priestly character of the ministry.

According to this interpretation, the sacerdotal terms in question are applied by S. Clement, as proper designations of the Christian ministry. If, however, it could be proved, what the advocates of the Presbyter theory urge, that the terms are here used only by analogy, yet the passage evidently implies an analogy of the closest and most intimate kind; the terms being employed without any guarding, or limitation. One can hardly conceive it possible that an advocate of the Presbyter theory should have used the terms, without some intimation to guard against the otherwise inevitable conclusion, that the same idea was understood to be embodied in both ministries. S. Clement was the disciple and companion of S. Paul, and his epistles are the purest and earliest evidence we can obtain, second only to that of the New Testament itself.

We have thus traced the idea of a sacerdotal ministry, together with the correlative ideas of altar, offerings, sacrifices, &c., in one unbroken line, up to the very age

[1] Editio tertia, denuo recognita. Oxonii, e typographeo Academico, 1847.

of inspiration. We have also seen that at least from the second century, the term, Priest, in its sacerdotal sense, was applied as the common distinctive appellation of the Christian minister; that during the first century it was thus applied, though not so commonly; and that there are even grounds for believing, that it was used from the beginning as the official name of the celebrant in the sacred offices of the Church. We have moreover seen, that the opposite view of the Jewish elder being the prototype of the Christian minister, arose only within the last three hundred years, as the justification and instrument of a schism, invented by one who was forced by his position to form a system independent of an ordained ministry; and this as part of a line of teaching which avowedly cast off all allegiance to primeval tradition, and to the Church, as "the keeper and witness of Holy Writ;" and, further, that this schismatical theory, when it was propounded, was rejected by our Reformers, and has uniformly been rejected by the Church of England, in spite of violent persecutions specially raised on account of the disputed doctrine, and with many inducements and much disposition on the part of some for peace' sake to surrender it, but resisted with the greater energy and determination, as increasing years showed more and more clearly its unsoundness and evil consequences.[1]

[1] The Presbyterian system of the preaching elder and the ruling elder, is grounded on 1 Tim. v. 17: "Let the elders that rule well be counted worthy of double honour, especially they who labour in the Word and doctrine." It is an uncatholic system, inasmuch as it makes spiritual authority to be a lay function, but far more so, because it ignores everything in Holy Scripture, which represents the Christian minister as being by his ordination the consecrated instrument or channel of Divine grace.

CHAPTER VIII.

TESTIMONY OF THE HOLY SCRIPTURES.

THE most momentous part of our inquiry yet remains; for unless the conclusions at which we have arrived, are found to be in accordance with the Word of GOD, there has been some error in the process of the investigation. But supposing no doubt to exist as to the doctrine of the Church, and believing that, according to the promise of the HOLY GHOST vouchsafed on the day of Pentecost, a doctrine so universally received from the beginning, can be none other than the voice of GOD, we may expect to find our conclusions verified in the Divine revelations. There must of necessity be entire accordance between the teaching of the Catholic Church and Holy Scripture, in order to constitute any doctrine the truth of GOD, and so binding on the soul.

It may seem to militate against the teaching of the Church, that the term Priest (ἱερεύς) is not applied in the New Testament to the Christian minister, but only to our LORD Himself, and to the members of His Body in general. This is the very stronghold of the Presbyter theory. The real question, however, it must be borne in mind, is not whether the ancient name was then so applied, for we have seen that it has been the usage of Holy Scripture, especially when a new dispensation was given, as was the case also among the heathen, to adopt fresh names and clothe them with fresh meanings,—but whether the *idea* of a Priesthood be not necessarily involved in the Scriptural representation of the Christian ministry, and whether the same sacerdotal system of Divine service, which we have seen in after ages pervading the entire Catholic Communion, was not in active operation during the period of the New Testament history, even from the Day of Pentecost. The reasons which may be suggested for the temporary disuse of the term in question, will hereafter be considered. It is sufficient here to observe, that the fact of a true Priesthood attaching to Christians generally, is in no respect incompatible with the doctrine of a true ministerial Priesthood; for the Israelites were all priests, while yet the separate consecration of the sons of Aaron was always definitively marked. (Comp. 1 S. Pet. ii. 9 with Ex. xix. 6.) Nor again is the application of the term to our Blessed LORD, as in a special manner the Priest of the New Testament a contradiction to the idea of a continued line of Priests following His Advent, any more than it was a contradiction to the fact of a line of Priests preceding it. A Priesthood to carry on His work of atonement, may be as truly a part of the Divine purpose, as a Priesthood " to prepare the way of the LORD."

Even in the case of our LORD it is the idea, not the then accustomed name of Priest, which is urged as of such vital importance. S. Paul contrasts our LORD with the ἱερεύς of the Old Testament under a new name which has ever belonged to the Christian Priest, that of λειτουργός, or celebrant. "We have such an high Priest, who is set on the right hand of the throne of the Majesty in the heavens; a minister of the sanctuary (τῶν ἁγίων λειτουργός), and of the true tabernacle, which the LORD pitched, and not man . . . . For if He were on earth, He should not be a Priest (ἱερεύς), seeing that those are Priests that offer gifts according to the law, who serve unto the example and shadow of heavenly things."[1] And again; "And now hath He obtained a more excellent ministry (λειτουργίας), by how much also He is the Mediator of a better covenant."[1] The old name, ἱερεύς, is for the occasion discarded, that it may make way for the coming in of the higher idea of a truer priesthood, and be disengaged from the shadowy typical characteristics of the Levitical idea of the Priest. And to mark the difference another and a new name is given.

That the idea of a ministerial Priesthood exists in the Gospel, may be proved (1) from incidental notices; (2) from the terms of the ministerial commission, and (3) from direct statements.

Among the incidental notices which occur in the New Testament, the following may be mentioned. S. Paul, speaking of the support of the ministry, refers to the law which provided for the sons of Aaron. (1 Cor. ix. 13.) "Do ye not know, that they who minister about holy things, live of the things of the temple; and they who wait at the altar, are partakers with the altar? Even so hath the LORD ordained, that they who preach the Gospel should live of the Gospel." Tithe is the homage of the world to a claim which has been felt to be grounded on the original grant of GOD to His Priests. Again, when

[1] Heb. viii. 1—5, and 6.

S. Paul speaks of the consequences of separation from the Christian ministry, the reference is to the same source, and the effect of schism under the Christian covenant is " the perishing in the gainsaying of Core." (S. Jude 11.)

Further, the symbolical language of the New Testament has been moulded after the same idea. Though the modes of interpreting the Book of Revelations have been very various; yet it is generally received as a principle of interpretation,—that the symbolic visions are heavenly representations of what takes place on earth. The opening vision (Rev. iv., v.) pictures forth the Church in the act of adoration. The assembled congregation of the elect are represented united in adoration with the ministry, under images manifestly borrowed from the temple. The Throne, and " He that sat upon it," is the Shekinah of the Holiest of all. "The seven lamps of fire," correspond with the seven-branched candlestick; "the sea of glass" with the brazen sea. " The altar of incense," and " the harps," the instrument used in the temple service, are parts of the same hallowed scene. The altar of sacrifice alone is wanting; but that could have had no place, where the very Lamb was Himself visible "in the midst of the Throne," " a Lamb as it had been slain." Around the Throne with these accompanying objects appear " the four and twenty Elders, clothed in white raiment." If these Elders, which here evidently represent the ministry, are the elders of the synagogue, they are transplanted from their proper sphere, and surrounded with all the elements of the temple service; and thus the passage proves the change which was passing over the idea of the Presbyter, and altering the meaning of the word. But it must be borne in mind that the number, twenty-four, corresponds with the number of courses into which the Aaronic Priests were divided; and each of those courses had a President, who was called "the Elder."[1] The Aaronic Priest, therefore, as well as the other elements of the temple, may have had his part in the imagery under which the Divine worship of the Christian Church is here symbolized.

There are other passages which, to a mind impressed with the traditionary teaching of the Church, appear equally to speak of a sacerdotal ministry and offices; although the interpretation is more doubtful, and therefore they cannot fairly be pressed in argument with an opponent. Such, e.g., is our LORD's mention of an altar,—"If thou bring thy gift to the altar," &c.;" (S. Matt. v. 23)—implying its continued existence in His Church; coupled with S. Paul's assertion of an exclusive altar with sacrifices to be fed upon, "We have an altar, whereof they have no right to eat, which serve the tabernacle." (Heb. xiii. 10.)[2] Again, when S.

---

[1] "Of priests, Zadock was the chief, of the family of Eleazar, and Ahimelech the second, of the family of Ithamar. (1 Chron. xxiv. 3.)

"Under these were twenty-four other courses, of the posterity of { Eleazar, sixteen, Ithamar, eight } 1 Chron. xxiv. 4, which twenty-four are called, in the fifth verse, rulers of the sanctuary, and rulers of the house of GOD: and to whom the learned interpreters think the twenty-four elders, Apoc. iv. 4, have relation, 'elders of the priests.' Jer. xix. 1; 2 Kings xix. 2." "A Summary View of the Government both of the Old and New Testament, by Bishop Andrewes."

[2] The same word (θυσιαστήριον) is used both for the Christian and Jewish altar alike in the New Testament, and for the altar of sacrifice, as well as the altar of incense, as in S. Luke xi. 51; Heb. vii. 13; 1

Paul is correcting the misuse of the gift of tongues among the Corinthians, and says; "Else when thou shalt bless with the Spirit, how shall he that occupieth the room of the unlearned, say Amen at thy giving of thanks, seeing he understandeth not what thou sayest?" (1 Cor. xiv. 14,) the allusion appears to be to some well known prayer, to which it was of the first importance that the congregation should be able to respond; and the prayer supposed to be alluded to, is the prayer of consecration in the Eucharistic Office, there being no other known prayer in which "blessing" and "giving thanks" are combined. If this be so, S. Paul is here speaking of that act of ministry, to which he had alluded previously in the same Epistle, as his own habitual office; "The cup of blessing which *we* bless, is it not the communion of the Blood of CHRIST?" (1 Cor. x. 16.) Again, when S. Paul, writing to the

Cor. ix. 13; x. 18. Schleusner says of the word: "Altare, locus in quo sacrificia et oblationes fiunt: a θυσιάζω, sacrificio, speciatim ara holocaustorum: Hebr. *mizbach*." The same word is commonly used in the Septuagint, as e.g. Gen. viii. 20; xii. 7, 8; xiii. 10. A different word, βωμός, is used in the New Testament in reference to heathen altars, as in Acts xvii. 23.

The passage from the Hebrews (v. 10) was interpreted to mean the altar of Christian sacrifice by Theodoret, Theophylact, and Œcumenius, among the Greeks, Primasius, Sedulius, and Anselm, among the Westerns; and they suppose the passage to correspond with 1 Cor. x. 21; "Ye cannot be partakers of the LORD's Table and the table of devils." S. Thomas Aquinas interpreted it of CHRIST crucified, i.e. the Victim Himself, and Estius prefers this interpretation. Modern commentators, equally as the ancient, are divided. Whichever interpretation is to be preferred, it is evident that the passage could not have been interpreted by any to refer to the altar of sacrifice in the Church, unless such an altar was believed to exist. So that the very dispute proves the existence of a real Christian sacrifice.

Romans, dwells on the grace that is given to him as an Apostle, he uses throughout terms of Priesthood; "that I should be the minister (λειτουργόν, lit. a Priest, so used, itself or its derivatives, Heb. viii. 2, 6; ix. 21; x. 11; S. Luke i. 23) of JESUS CHRIST to the Gentiles, ministering (ἱερουργοῦντα, lit. as a Priest) the Gospel of GOD, that the offering up (προσφορά, a sacrificial offering) of the Gentiles might be acceptable, being sanctified (again a sacrificial term, ἡγιασμένη) by the HOLY GHOST. (Rom. xv. 16.)[1]

A most important passage, however, which is not open to the doubts attaching to the texts alluded to, occurs in S. Paul's Epistle to the Corinthians, where the Apostle urges the necessity of entire separation from idol worship. The words employed evidently show the identity of the principle of heathen and Christian sacrifices, while yet they assert their entire distinctness of object and effect, the same terms being used as equally applicable in both cases. It cannot be supposed that language, so liable to convey a false impression on vital doctrine, would have been employed, unless the idea of sacrifice, and consequently that of Priesthood, were truly applicable to the Christian system. The words occur immediately after S. Paul's allusion to the "cup of blessing" and "the bread which we

---

[1] Vitringa feels the weight of this text, admitting "that the Apostle here refers to the prophecy of Isaiah" (lxvi. 21), and that the passage certainly marks the existence of a Priesthood in the Christian Church: but he gets over the difficulty by supposing it to refer not to the ministry, but to the exercise of priestly powers by the people at large. It is evident however that S. Paul is here speaking not of the people, but of himself as an Apostle: "the grace that is given unto *me* of GOD, that I should be," &c.

break," and are as follows: "Behold Israel after the flesh: are not they which eat of the sacrifices, partakers of the altar? What say I, then? that the idol is anything, or that which is offered in sacrifice to idols is anything? But I say that the things which the Gentiles sacrifice, they sacrifice to devils, and not to GOD; and I would not that ye should have fellowship with devils. Ye cannot drink the Cup of the LORD and the cup of devils: ye cannot be partakers of the LORD's Table, and the table of devils." (1 Cor. x. 18—21.)

Here the table and cup of devils are opposed to the Table and Cup of the LORD: sacrifice to devils to sacrifice to GOD; fellowship with devils to fellowship with the LORD. The terms are opposed as falsehood to truth; but the very comparison implies in both cases one idea common to mankind in reference to sacrifice and union with GOD. It was the prevailing notion that the demon was personally, though invisibly, present at the feast, a dark and awful type of a real Truth which is our continual blessing in the Church of GOD; and that partaking of the feast was a real union with the supposed Deity, equally a type of our mysterious bliss in the Holy Eucharist. This heathen notion S. Paul represents as a perverted, but still an exact, image of a great and real mystery,—that what the heathen worshipper supposed to be the object and end of his sacrifice, is realised in its Truth in ours. That even the Jewish sacrifices are represented by S. Paul in this passage only as emblematic of our ever present Blessing, is thus brought out by S. Chrysostom in his comment on v. 18: "But do thou, I pray, consider how, with regard to the Jews, he said not 'They are partakers with GOD,' but *they are partakers of the altar;* for what was placed thereon was burnt: but in respect to the Body of CHRIST, not so. But how? It is *the Communion of the Lord's Body.* For not of the altar, but of CHRIST Himself, are we made partakers."

The singular prominence which the Holy Eucharist obtained from the beginning, has a very important bearing on our inquiry. It has been shown how this mystical service formed the central and fundamental idea of Divine Worship in the Early Church. This was equally true during the time when the New Testament was written. The Acts of the Apostles open with the following scene of the Church's earliest worship: "And they continued steadfastly in the Apostles' doctrine and fellowship, and in (the) breaking of (the) bread, (τῇ κλάσει τοῦ ἄρτου,) and in prayer." (ch. ii. 42.) The combination of Eucharist and prayer corresponds with that of sacrifice and prayer, which marked the commencement of patriarchal worship. That the Eucharist should thus at once become the leading feature in the worship of the Church, is readily accounted for, when we consider that it is the only service which our LORD commanded, and which Himself first celebrated. It is the one essential act of worship which He personally ordained as the vital bond between Himself and His Church. In "the upper chamber," "the same night that He was betrayed," there were revealed the outline, the main features, and, it may be far more than we are in the least aware, the very words of the Church's undying liturgies. Whatever passed that night must have been fixed indelibly in the minds of the Apostles, and was through them by the SPIRIT transfused into the living action of the Church. Nor is it difficult, even after this lapse of time, to trace out the points of resemblance in our own Eucharistic service. The long discourses recorded by S. John, the intercessory prayer, and the hymn that was sung, are perpetuated in the readings of Scripture, the sermon, the lengthened intercessions, and the singing of hymns, which have always formed parts of the liturgy, the 'blessing' and 'giving of thanks' being then, as now, its central features.

What words our LORD used, as He took the bread and the wine, and "blessed," and "gave thanks," and offered Himself to the FATHER, are not recorded, though they could not have escaped the notice of the Apostles, and were no doubt among the remembrances which the HOLY GHOST recalled to their minds. We may even now be using, unknowingly, our LORD's own words of blessing, oblation, and thanksgiving, even as we use His words of consecration.

Nor is it of little moment to our inquiry to observe, that the original words, translated in our version, "Do this in remembrance of Me," had in the ears of a Jew a fixed meaning, long hallowed in the usage of the people, as connected with sacrifice. "Do ($ποιεῖτε$) this," in the language of the Septuagint, means, as it meant among heathen writers, "offer as a sacrifice."[1] So also the term

---

[1] For this use of the term in the Septuagint, see, among numberless passages, Exod. xxix. 36—39; Lev. vi. 22; ix. 7, where it is translated in our version "offer;" Exod. x. 25, where it is translated "sacrifice;" Lev. iv. 20, where it is translated, as in the Gospels, "do,"—"He shall do with ($ποιήσει$) the bullock (i.e. offer) as he did with ($ἐποίησε$, lit. offered) the bullock for a sin-offering." As applied specially to the

"in remembrance of Me," (εἰς τὴν ἐμὴν ἀνάμνησιν,) or rather, "for a memorial of Me," is sacrificial; the memorial in a sacrifice being that portion of the Victim which is laid on the altar and offered to GOD, in order to bring the whole oblation to remembrance before

Passover, see Numb. ix. 2; Deut. xvi. 1; 2 Kings xxiii. 21; 2 Chron. xxx. 1, 2; xxxv. 1; Ezra vi. 19, where it is translated "keep" or celebrate. S. Paul uses the term, Heb. xi. 28, "Through faith he kept (ἐποίησε, offered) the Passover and sprinkling of blood, lest He that destroyed the firstborn should touch them." Compare also S. Luke ii. 27, where simply "to do (ποιῆσαι) after the custom of the law," corresponds with v. 24, "to offer a sacrifice (δοῦναι θυσίαν) according to that which is said in the Law of the LORD." Throughout the Septuagint ποιεῖν is used as synonymous with ἱεροποιεῖν or ἱερουργεῖν. It is used also for dressing or preparing the sacrifice, as in Lev. vii. 9, 10, &c., &c.

A friend has suggested to the Author that the use of these sacrificial terms may explain the much-questioned passage; Gen. iv. 7. "If thou doest (προσενέγκῃς LXX.) well, shalt thou not be accepted? and if thou doest not well, sin lieth at the door:" in other words, "If thou offerest the appointed sacrifice, shalt thou not be accepted, as Abel? if thou offerest not the appointed sacrifice, the opportunity of redeeming the error, the true sacrifice of expiation, is ready at hand."

The corresponding Latin word, "facere," had the same meaning; and as ποιεῖν was used by the Greek Fathers to denote the oblation in the Eucharist, so "missam facere" was the phrase commonly used to express the same by the Latin Fathers. "Facere" in the Vulgate is the version of ποιεῖν in the Septuagint, and both correspond with "do" in our version. (See Hickes, c. ii. s. 7.)

S. Chrysostom contrasts the Sacrifice of the Passover with that of the Holy Eucharist, and employs the same word in both cases to express the offering. "See how he weans and draws them from Jewish rites: 'For,' says he, 'as ye offered that (i.e. the Passover, ἐκεῖνο ἐποιεῖτε) in remembrance of the miraculous deliverance from Egypt, so offer (ποιεῖτε) this in remembrance of Me: that blood was shed for the preservation of the first-born, this for the remission of the sins of the whole world." (S. Chrysost. on S. Matt. xxvi., lxxxii.)

Him. (See Levit. ii. 2, 9.)[1] The idea implied is not that of an act of memory on the part of man, but a memorializing of GOD.

It must be considered, moreover, that the institution of the Blessed Sacrament was commanded to the Apostles as a new Passover. The Paschal Lamb had been eaten in token that the dispensation of the Law had reached its close, and our LORD took the bread and wine which remained after the feast, to make of them the materials of a new sacrifice,—a new system arising out of the ruins of the old. He delivered Himself openly unto death before the eyes of the disciples, under the external forms of the elements, which He thus assumed, and then gave Himself to them as their Food. "And the bread which I will give is My Flesh, which I will give for the life of the world." The mystery at once took the form of a sacrifice; and the truest, as well as the simplest, comment on the history of the whole transaction is to be found in the words of S. Cyprian: "If JESUS, our LORD and GOD, is the High Priest of GOD the FATHER, and first offered Himself a sacrifice to the FATHER, and commanded that this should be done in remembrance of Him, doth not he who doeth as CHRIST did, truly act as a Priest in the place of CHRIST, and then offer a true and proper sacrifice in the Church to

[1] μνημόσυνον is the word used in Levit. ii. ; but ἀνάμνησις is used in a similar sense in Numb. x. 10, and Levit. xxiv. 7. In this latter place it is used in reference to the shewbread, which has been considered to be specially a type of the Eucharistic elements. The only place where ἀνάμνησις is used in the New Testament besides its use in the institution of the Eucharist, is Heb. x. 3, and there also it expresses the idea of a commemoration made before GOD, and not a remembrance in a man's own mind.

God the Father, when he offers in the same manner in which he may perceive Christ Himself offered?" (Epist. lxiii. ad Cæcil.)

2. We have hitherto considered only partial or incidental passages touching the ministry and its services. The terms of the Apostolic commission are, however, the most complete guide to the determination of the question. As in the Old, so in the New Testament, the ministerial commission was not given in one formal statement, but is to be gathered from the scattered notices which occur in the course of the Revelation. These notices, when brought together, fall under the following heads; and it is to be observed how closely the Apostolic commission, both in its general scope and in its details, coincides with that of the sons of Aaron:—

APOSTOLIC COMMISSION.	AARONIC.
ADMISSION TO THE COVENANT.	
By Holy Baptism. "Go ye and teach (lit. make disciples of) all nations, baptizing them in the Name of the Father, and of the Son, and of the Holy Ghost." (S. Matt. xxviii. 19.)	*The offerings appointed after childbirth, and for the redemption of the first-born in connection with the rite of Circumcision.*
AUTHORITATIVE TEACHING.	
"Teaching them to observe all things whatsoever I have commanded you." (S. Matt. xxviii. 20.)	"The Priest's lips should keep knowledge, and the people should seek the Law at their mouth." (Mal. ii. 7.)
JUDGMENT IN CONTROVERSY.	
"He that heareth you, heareth Me." (S. Luke x. 16.)	"And the Priests the sons of Levi shall come near ... and by

APOSTOLIC COMMISSION.

"If he neglect to hear the Church, let him be unto thee as a heathen man and a publican." (S. Matt. xviii. 17.)

"The Council of Jerusalem." (Acts xv. 6.)

AARONIC.

their word shall every controversy and every stroke be tried."

ECCLESIASTICAL RULE.

"Whatsoever ye shall bind on earth shall be bound in heaven: and whatsoever ye shall loose on earth shall be loosed in heaven." (S. Matt. xviii. 18.)

"According to the sentence of the Law which they shall teach thee, and according to the judgment which they shall tell thee, thou shalt do: thou shalt not decline from the sentence which they shall show thee, to the right hand nor to the left. And the man that will do presumptuously, and will not hearken to the Priest that standeth to minister there before the LORD thy GOD, or unto the judge, even that man shall die, and thou shalt put away the evil from Israel." (Deut. xvii. 11, 12.)

RECONCILIATION AND EXCOMMUNICATION.

"Receive ye the HOLY GHOST: Whosesoever sins ye remit, they are remitted; and whosesoever sins ye retain, they are retained." (S. John xx. 22, 23.)

"And all things are of GOD, Who hath reconciled us unto Himself, and hath given unto us the ministry of reconciliation." (2 Cor. v. 18.)

"For though I should boast somewhat more of our authority,

"The Priest shall look on him, and pronounce him unclean." (Lev. xiii. 8, 11, 20, 22, 25, 30—44.)

"The Priest shall pronounce him clean." (Lev. xiii. 6, 17, 23, 28, 34.)

"The Priest that maketh him clean." (Lev. xiv. 11.)

APOSTOLIC COMMISSION.

which the LORD hath given us for edification and not for your destruction, I should not be ashamed." (2 Cor. x. 8; 1 Tim. i. 20.)

AARONIC.

OFFERING SACRIFICES AND OTHER OBLATIONS.

"This do (ποιεῖτε) in remembrance of Me." (1 Cor. xi. 25.)

"This do ye (ποιεῖτε), as often as ye drink it, in remembrance of Me." (1 Cor. xi. 25.) N.B.—The same word (ποιεῖν) is used here, and translated " do," which is used in the contrasted passage of Leviticus, and translated "offer."

"And Moses said unto Aaron, Go unto the altar and offer (ποίησον) thy sin offering and thy burnt offering, and make an atonement for thyself and for the people, and offer (ποίησον) the offering of the people, and make an atonement for them as the LORD commanded." (Lev. ix. 7.)

INTERCESSION.

"Is any sick among you? Let him call for the elders of the Church; and let them pray over him, anointing him with oil in the Name of the LORD; and the prayer of faith shall save the sick, and the LORD shall raise him up; and if he have committed sins, they shall be forgiven him." (S. James v. 14, 15.)

"And Moses said unto Aaron, Take a censer, and put fire therein from off the altar, and put on incense, and go quickly unto the Congregation, and make an atonement for them; for there is wrath gone out from the LORD, the plague is begun . . . . And he stood between the living and the dead, and the plague was stayed." (Numb. xvi. 46, 48.)

BENEDICTION.

"The grace of the LORD JESUS CHRIST, and the love of GOD, and the Communion of the HOLY GHOST, be with you all. Amen." (2 Cor. xiii. 14.)

"Speak unto Aaron and his sons, saying, On this wise ye shall bless the children of Israel, saying unto them, The LORD bless thee and keep thee: the LORD make His face to shine upon thee, and

APOSTOLIC COMMISSION. AARONIC.

be gracious unto thee. The LORD lift up His countenance upon thee, and give thee peace." (Numb. vi. 23—26.)

The two ministries are obviously co-extensive, covering corresponding spheres of action, and moving along similar lines, which converge and meet all at one centre. The one precedes, the other succeeds, the Sacrifice of the SON of GOD; the one is the instrument of the typical, prefigurative Law, the other of its antitype and fulfilment. GOD in both cases appointed the mode whereby He would be approached. The Law contained in its ordinances the types and "shadows of good things to come," and "not the very image of the things." (Heb. x. 1.) The Church, which is the temple of the HOLY GHOST, the very "Body of CHRIST," contains in its rites and ministries the "image" itself,—the living form in which the Substance is enshrined, through which It breathes and imparts Itself.[1] Not that the things done

---

[1] The term "image," as contrasted with "shadow," is used in Scripture to denote 'a living form, having a real, substantial existence.' Thus it is used to express our Blessed LORD'S Personality in the flesh: "CHRIST, Who is the image of GOD," (2 Cor. iv. 4): "the express image of His Person" (Heb. i. 3). And, again, it is applied to the living body of man: "As we have borne the image of the earthy, we shall also bear the image of the heavenly." (1 Cor. xv. 49.) As applied to ordinances, it means outward forms which contain grace, as their substance and life, in contradistinction to mere types or signs, as the Jewish ordinances were. This distinction is made by S. Paul between Jewish and Christian ordinances. (Heb. x. 1.) The Fathers employed the word as noting the distinction between the Jewish rites on the one hand, and the full blessedness of unveiled glory in heaven on the other. Thus S. Ambrose speaks of Jewish rites as the "shadow," Christian sacraments the "image," and future glory the "truth."

in the Church are formed upon the model of the Law of Moses, they are rather the embodiments and organs of those "heavenly things unto the example and shadow" of which the rites of the Law served. The Law was a copy of existing realities in the heavens, and those very realities have now assumed a body in which they live, and through which they manifest themselves. The ministries of the Church not merely express and image forth, they contain and convey, what the rites of the Law shadowed. Signs are become sacraments. The one all-sufficient Sacrifice is not, as of old, typified, but is commemorated in the Oblation of the Church, and its substance is "verily and indeed given." "The Law was given by Moses, but grace and truth came by JESUS CHRIST." Is it possible that they who ministered those carnal ordinances, "which could not make him that did the service perfect, as pertaining to the conscience," should be the real priests, and they who minister "through the offering of the Body of JESUS CHRIST once for all," have no priestly character?

Nor is this all. There are expressions which prove that the Apostolic ministry is co-extensive with that of our LORD Himself. When Scripture speaks of the Catholic Church as a household, the minister is the steward; and a steward, unlike the other servants, has entrusted to him all his unseen Master's goods, to be distributed through his hands. And Christian ministers are "stewards," not of the Word only, but "of the mysteries of GOD," which our Church, in unison with the Church Catholic, has understood to mean sacraments, in which is lodged the manifold grace of GOD. Again, when the Church is spoken of as a kingdom, the minister is the ambassador; and an ambassador, unlike all other ministers of the crown, is the complete representative of the unseen sovereign. The fulness of a delegated charge is implied in both expressions. The latter metaphor, more especially, implies a Priesthood in the ministry; for the very characteristic of our LORD's kingly character is, that He is "a Priest on His Throne." (Zech. vi. 13.) If, then, the priestly office were eliminated from the Apostolic commission, the very distinctiveness of CHRIST's kingdom would have no true representation upon earth, and His ministers could not be rightly termed "ambassadors for CHRIST." (2 Cor. v. 20.)

A remarkable intimation of the ministerial power about to be committed to human agency was given by our LORD in the act of absolving the "man sick of the palsy, lying on a bed." The mystery involved in His words, as He reasoned with the Scribes, was the delegation of the Divine gift of the pardon of sin to Himself as Man: "That ye may know, that the Son of Man" (the title specially distinguishing His Humanity) "hath power upon earth to forgive sins." It was the announcement of a new order of ministry arising through His Incarnation, to apply the gifts of Divine grace. The bystanders dimly perceived the amazing consequences of this new dispensation; or they unconsciously bore witness to the truth involved in our LORD's act as to the priestly commission to be bestowed through Him on men who should minister the same gifts among their brethren. "When the multitude saw it, they marvelled, and glorified GOD, which had given such power unto *men.*" (S. Matt. ix. 1—8.)

Moreover, the express words which preceded the solemn act of ordination are most conclusive as to the extent of the ministry then committed unto men. "As My FATHER hath sent Me, even so send I you. And when He had said this, He breathed on them," &c. (S. John xx. 22.) These words can admit no reservation of any characteristic part of our LORD's ministry. His mission was to be Prophet, Priest, and King. The kingly office is discharged by the exercise of ecclesiastical judgment and discipline; the prophetic by teaching. The priestly office must, in like manner, be dispensed by a subordinate human agency, or one essential part of the mission fails in its fulfilment. It is the more remarkable that there should be any doubt, whether the priestly office were committed unto men, when it is acknowledged that the regal and prophetic functions are so committed; because, when our LORD after His Resurrection, ordaining the Apostles, selected one special mark of their ministry to be expressed in words and thus openly sealed upon them, He chose not the office of ruling, nor that of teaching, though both are avowedly characteristic attributes of their ministry, but He chose for special mention that one branch which of necessity involves a priestly character, viz., that of the remission of sins: "Whosesoever sins ye remit, they are remitted," &c.

Nor is it possible that these high terms should be limited to, and fulfilled in, the Apostles themselves; for our LORD accompanied the commission with the promise, "Lo, I am with you alway, even unto the end of the world." (S. Matt. xxviii. 20.) These words, from their connection with the commission preceding them evidently applying to an earthly ministry, could not be fulfilled in the persons of the Apostles, but only in the successive line of an order which was to take its rise from them, and perpetuate their being on the earth to the end of time. Again, if these high terms do not apply still, but had their fulfilment in the lifetime of the Apostles, then it would follow that there is now no Divine mission of a ministry in the Church at all. The alternative lies between the full Apostolic commission, and congregationalism; between the one Divine and a simply human organisation. But English Churchmen, at least, cannot doubt the living and perpetual application of the Apostolic commission, because in our Ordinal we employ the very words used by our LORD, when He breathed on the Apostles, as our form of commission, with the awful accompaniment, "Receive ye the HOLY GHOST," which would be blasphemy, if it were not true, according to the universal tradition of the Church, that Holy Orders are sacramental, conferring grace for the work committed; and that every fresh ordination is an ever-renewed act of CHRIST Himself.

The distinction between the extraordinary and the ordinary, the temporary and the abiding elements in the Apostolic commission, need be no difficulty. For a simple rule has ever guided the mind of the Church in this respect, viz., that whatever concerns the welfare of souls and the communication of grace, is ordinary, and to abide for ever; but that gifts or powers external to the soul are not necessarily conveyed by the terms of the commission. To use Jeremy Taylor's words, where he is speaking of the power of inflicting diseases and death, which the Apostles possessed, in "binding" sinners, or on the contrary, healing sicknesses in "absolving" them,—"It was in this, as in all other ministries, something miraculous and extraordinary was for ever to consign a lasting truth and ministry in ordinary."[1] If any function of the ministry concerns the peace and life of souls, it is the means of reconciliation and communion with GOD, and must therefore fall under the head of ordinary ministrations. And these are the very points involved in the idea of a priestly commission.

Taking the Holy Scriptures, then, as our guide,—by many incidental notices, by symbolical as well as direct statements, by the terms of the commission, and the special prominence given to the idea of a ministry of reconciliation and forgiveness of sins,—by our LORD's associating His ministers with Himself in the Eucharistic Oblation, and by the co-extensiveness of the Apostolic mission with that of our LORD, which commission has descended in its fulness along the line of the ministry of the Catholic and Apostolic Church,— we conclude that ministers who inherit this grace are endued, not merely with functions of spiritual rule and authority to teach, but are also, in Jeremy Taylor's words, "ministers of CHRIST's Priesthood," and thus themselves, in Him, true Priests.

[1] Jeremy Taylor's Treatise on Repentance. Of Ecclesiastical Penance, sect. iv. 49.

CHAPTER IX.

THE PRINCIPLE OF PRIESTHOOD.

IT will tend to elucidate the subject, and also confirm the conclusions at which we have arrived, if we consider the root or essential principle of a sacerdotal ministry, i.e. that which specially distinguishes a Priest from other ministers in the things of GOD.

The slaughter of an animal victim in sacrifice is not, as some have supposed, the essential characteristic of a Priest; for by the Levitical Law it was appointed that the victim should be put to death, not by the Priest, but by the worshipper (see Lev. i. 2, 5). In later years the custom grew for the Levites, or subordinate attendants, to slay and prepare the victim. (See 2 Chron. xxix. 24, 34.) The Priest's office was to offer on the altar, sprinkle the blood, and distribute the consecrated food of the sacrifice.

Nor again were sacrifices of blood essential to a true Priesthood. Hickes (lib. 11, sec. iv.) has shown by a large collection of evidence, as e.g., from the customs of the early Romans and Persians, who had no animal sacrifices, and, in modern times, from the case of the Mahometans, that the ministers of such religions have been always regarded as true Priests. According to the

Levitical law the sin-offering of a poor man was bloodless, of fine flour only (Lev. v. 1—4); yet was it equally a true sacrifice, "to make atonement" for his sin. The material or nature of the offering therefore cannot be the determining point as to the character of a priestly ministry.

The laws which regulated the Levitical sacrifices, being evidently typical in all their details, give the true key to the principle which underlies the system in all its variations. In regard both to burnt-offerings, and sin-offerings offered by private individuals, the same general course of proceeding was ordained. The victim was brought before the door of the tabernacle, and the offerer laid his hand on the head of the victim, "that it might be accepted for him." By this act he symbolized the open acknowledgment of his sin before GOD, and of the justice of its appointed doom, together with a humble profession of faith in the true vicarious Sacrifice, upon Whom "the LORD hath laid the iniquities of us all." The victim was then taken by the offerer to the north side of the altar, and was there bled to death. By this was typified the acknowledgment of death being the proper desert of sin, and a pleading of the merits of the death of CHRIST, the north side being emblematic of the region and shadow of death in the natural world, and so of the miserable state to which sin had reduced mankind, into which the LORD voluntarily descended, that He might share it with us, and so redeem us from it. The Priest, and the Priest alone, received the blood of the victim, and sprinkled it upon the altar. This typified the act of absolution following upon the confession, with the application of the merits and virtues of

F

the most precious Blood of the true "Lamb of GOD, that taketh away the sins of the world." The principle was the same, when Aaron, taking his censer and burning incense therein, "stood between the living and the dead, and the plague was stayed" (Numb. xvi. 48); and again, when the life of Abimelech hung upon Abraham's prayer: "for he is a Prophet, and he shall pray for thee, and thou shalt live." (Gen. xv. 7.)

In all these cases alike, the intervention of the commissioned agent, applying the appointed means with the promises of a special covenant, was the principle on which the expected blessing depended; and it is this intervention which constituted the sacerdotal act. Grotius, therefore, in his commentary on Heb. ii. 17, has given the true definition of the Priest's office, founded on this deeper view of the subject. "It was the Priest's office," he says, "to be in GOD's stead (Dei vice fungi) to the people, and the people's stead (populi vice) to GOD." Estius, commenting on ch. viii. ver. 6 of the Epistle to the Hebrews, gives the same definition, though in fuller detail: "It is the office of a priest to mediate between GOD and men, to confirm compacts between them by offering sacrifice, and by his offices to provide that men become partakers of the Divine promises." Again, Hickes, in his "Christian Priesthood Asserted," (chap. ii., sec. 1,) expresses the same idea, grounding it on S. Paul's statement (Heb. v. 1), when he describes a Priest, as one who "among men stands in the presence of GOD to perform Divine offices for them, and for their benefit and good, to reconcile them to GOD and GOD to them, or to obtain graces and favours to them from Him, and as it were to interpose between Him and them."

Mediation, or ministerial intervention between GOD and man, is in all these statements represented to be the principle of Priesthood. A Priest is one who, not by any merit, or virtue, or power of his own, but by the will of GOD, has been made a necessary link in the chain-work of the Divine purposes. Himself as ineffectual as the words he speaks, or the inanimate creatures he may employ in his ministrations, he has nevertheless received, no necessary superiority indeed over his fellow men, but an attribute of grace, distinct from them, though given for their sakes, by virtue of which they are brought into such relationship with GOD, that through his instrumentality, they obtain the promised blessings of the covenant under which they live. His office has a twofold aspect; on the one hand, the acts of his brethren through him become acceptable with GOD, and through him, on the other hand, the acts of GOD reach unto them.

The doctrine of the Priesthood can be no difficulty to one who considers the law of intermediate causes prevailing throughout the creation of GOD. Among the manifold forces of nature, no one can act alone. Each needs the presence of other agents, or certain fixed conditions must co-exist, before its powers can operate. The powers of vegetation, e.g. need the presence of light for their true development. The co-existence of vegetable life is necessary for the sustenance of animal life. The acting of various external circumstances, again, on the formation of the human frame and character, is one of the most prominent facts of physiology.

It has pleased the Creator thus to limit by certain laws His own operations, and to make the infinite outgoings of His will dependent on the presence and actings of His own creatures. The spiritual world is no exception to this all pervading principle of mutual interdependence and conditional instrumentality.

The law of intervention specially characterizes the Gospel. This vital principle pervades the central truth of the Incarnation of GOD: for the Incarnation is the assumption of the Humanity, in order to become a medium of communication between GOD and man. GOD willed not to act on man directly, but through the intervention of the human nature in CHRIST. "In Him dwelleth all the fulness of the Godhead bodily," and from Him flow forth all the gifts that GOD has willed to impart to man. They flow, not directly from GOD, but indirectly through the Manhood of CHRIST. It is the same principle of interposition which characterizes priestly attributes in created natures; the essential difference being, that in CHRIST the principle of Priesthood exists as a self-originated attribute, inherent and independent of all others. And therefore the Fathers distinguished Him among all His brethren, as ὁ μόνος φύσει ἀρχιερεύς, "the only High Priest by nature;" in the same sense in which Holy Scripture distinguishes Him, as the "One Mediator between GOD and man;" while yet they held that the operations of his Priesthood and Mediation were extended from Him through subordinate and dependent agents to the redeemed world.

Our LORD Himself, on many occasions, showed how this law of intervention was not to be limited to His own Person, but that His purpose was to associate His creatures with Himself in the exercise of His mediatorial functions. When "He spat on the ground, and made clay of the spittle, and anointed the eyes of the blind man with the clay, and said, Go, wash in the pool of Siloam" (S. John ix. 6) ; even in this act of proving Himself the " Light of the world," He invested the lowest creatures with the power of communicating this precious gift. In raising the dead, an act in which, above all others, it might have seemed no creature could have any share with GOD, there must yet be intermediate agents. One who stands by must " take away the stone," before the Dead can come forth ; and others must "loose him and let him go," before he can be free. (S. John xi. 39, 44.) A yet more apposite instance of the truth here sought to be established, occurs in the two remarkable miracles of feeding the many thousands with the few loaves. " JESUS took the loaves, and gave thanks ;" but they were distributed by " the disciples to them that were set down." (S. John vi. 11.) In these cases human instrumentality was employed, not merely, as in the case of the raising of Lazarus, in the accidental accompaniments of the miracle, but in the miracle itself; for even in passing through the hands of the Apostles the bread mysteriously grew, and was multiplied according to the need of the recipients. The miracle was evidently symbolical, and when immediately afterwards our LORD spoke of giving His Flesh and Blood for the life of the world, it suggests itself as an inference involved in the type, that this true Bread, His very Body, would pass miraculously through human hands.

It must be borne in mind, moreover, that the intervention of a human ministry, to bring into act, and extend to mankind, the Priesthood of our LORD, is only one portion of a vast sacramental system. It has been the uniform teaching of the Church, that CHRIST ordained sacraments, whereby to communicate the graces of His Redemption. "The Church and the Sacraments are, like man himself, compounded of body and spirit; and the body of them, though inferior and for the sake of the spirit, is yet so necessary, that it is made by GOD to be the instrument and channel of His gifts: so that, except through their outward parts, we can neither possess ordinarily, nor even conceive or name, the distinctions and relations of spiritual things." The same Will which ordained that through the intervention of water and the Sacred Name regeneration should be vouchsafed, and that bread and wine should become the Body and Blood of CHRIST our LORD, has willed also, as part of the same system, that an order of men, "taken from among men, should be ordained for men," to be the agents in this system of instrumentality, and so fellow-workers with GOD. Sacerdotal mediation is a necessary correlative of sacraments, and is itself sacramental.

Moreover, the principles already stated show what constitutes a true Priesthood, and wherein its strength lies. A true Priesthood is one ordained of GOD; for no man "taketh this honour unto himself, but he that is called of GOD, as was Aaron." And the strength of a Priesthood lies in the closeness of its relation to the One Mediator. The Priests of the heathen world bear witness to the efficacy of human mediation, themselves possessing no efficacy. In its commencement, idolatry assumed a power which was given only to the Patriarchal line; and now, still a mere shadow, it bears a world-wide evidence to the reality of a true dispensation of GOD. The truth and efficacy of the Patriarchal and Aaronic Priesthoods rested on their being the only ordained types of our LORD. Their life hung on this connection. When, therefore, the Jewish Priests rejected CHRIST, by that very act they sealed the doom of their order, and ceased to be true Priests, as their sacrifices ceased to be acceptable sacrifices. They continued their ministrations during many years, unconscious, as Samson, that their strength had departed from them; but it was only the mechanical clinging to forms of which the life had all passed away, as ghosts are thought to linger still amidst the ruins of their former glory. The Jewish Priests became thenceforward the untrue shadows of their former selves, as the Priests of the heathen had been of their progenitors of the Patriarchal line. They lingered on awhile, as Balaam standing beside "the seven altars and the seven rams;" their prayers and their imprecations alike utterly rejected, while yet they gave to the world an unwilling testimony to a mystery of love now resting on another race.

The ordination of the Apostles instantly followed the completion of the act which involved the rejection of the Levitical Priesthood. Our LORD ordained them on His return from the grave. On his first reappearance among the twelve, "then said JESUS unto them, Peace be unto you. As My FATHER hath sent Me, even so send I you," &c. They had before been "called." (S. Matt. x. 1.) It had been already foretold that the keys of the kingdom of heaven should be given unto them (S. Matt. xvi. 19); but till that hour the keys of the kingdom were in other hands. Moreover the powers of ordination had been conveyed in part in the commission to offer the Eucharistic sacrifice, and from that hour therefore dates the most momentous attribute of the Apostolic ministry; but it was not then complete. It was when the apostasy of the Jewish Priesthood was accomplished in the crucifixion of the LORD of glory, that another Priesthood arose in its fulness. It was still the same ministry, if viewed as to its essential life; for both the Levitical and the Christian ministries lived through the relationship which GOD had formed between them and His Blessed SON,—the one, a Priesthood of hope in Him Who was to come, the other, a Priesthood of faith in Him Who was present. Only there was this momentous distinction in favour of the Christian Priesthood, that, through CHRIST's Presence abiding in the Flesh, the relation was become more intimate; and, not figuratively, or in manner of speech, but by distinct promise and covenant, never made before, an identity of ministration was established between Himself and His ministers, Himself accompanying them in their service,—"LO, I AM WITH YOU always,"—so that their acts, if done under the prescribed conditions, are His acts; their sacrifice, His sacrifice of Himself; their distribution, His communion of His Flesh and Blood; their absolutions and benedictions, His voice of pardon and peace.

This view of the sacramental character of the Christian Priesthood serves to explain the language of the Fathers, which to many appears hyperbolical and unreal. They who habitually realized the Invisible Presence in visible forms, understood in a literal sense such Scriptural words as these: " He that receiveth you, receiveth Me;

and he that receiveth Me, receiveth Him that sent Me."[1] They understood how CHRIST had vouchsafed to borrow from the creature place and time and instrumental agency, as the modes of His Presence and His actings; and therefore it was in them natural to look on the ordained symbols and instruments, as the embodiments of CHRIST Himself. S. Ignatius could use the following words, not as a singular instance, but as his habitual manner of speech; (Ep. ad Smyrnæos, c. viii.) "Flee divisions, as the root of evil. Let all follow the Bishop, as JESUS CHRIST the FATHER: and the Presbytery, as the Apostles; and reverence the deacons, as the ordinance of GOD." And again S. Polycarp; (Ep. ad Philip. v.) "Be subject to the Presbyters and Deacons, as to GOD and CHRIST."

Long bitter controversies and multiplied divisions, chilling love, and undermining the life of faith; habits of subjectiveness of thought, withdrawing the soul from the contemplation of the Invisible; above all, sins in the Priesthood itself—have marred both the vividness and the simplicity of a belief once intensely realized. Ages of coldness and infidelity have drifted us away from the land of visions, most real and deeply consoling, in which the forefathers of our faith once lived, and have separated the Invisible from the visible, explaining away into metaphor and hyperbole expressions of Holy Scripture itself, which undoubtedly identify the sign and the thing signified, those who are sent with Him Who sends them.

Yet the covenant stands unrepealed, and "the gifts and calling of GOD are without repentance." The com-

[1] S. Matt. x. 40.

mission of the ministry, and the results of a participation in its appointed acts, are the same now as at the beginning. It is still, and must continue to be, even to the end, the only ordained means of bringing out into effect the virtues of the Death and Passion of CHRIST; the consecrated channel of communication through which in CHRIST GOD and man, heaven and earth, are made one. Nor is it only High Church doctrine which involves the necessity of a Priesthood. Whatever may be the precise definition of such doctrines, as Absolution, or the Real Presence in the Blessed Sacrament, yet if it be held that the act of the minister is in any real sense essential by Divine appointment in order to the reception of the blessing sought, and that the faith of the receiver is not the only condition, the minister must in such case be held to be a Priest. Ministerial intervention constitutes the priestly nature of the act. And the promise of GOD binding the inward grace to the ministration, constitutes it a priestly service of a true and life-giving character.

The only possible view of Christianity, according to which there is no Priesthood, is that which represents Absolution simply as preaching, or reading aloud general promises of mercy, which any one may read for himself; and the Eucharist as a mere commemorative rite, the benefit of which depends simply on the act of the receiver's mind. One proof of this assertion is to be found in the uniform history of language; for wherever the sacramental idea of the Church has been broken down, the term "Priest" has been discarded, as no longer appropriate in the conscience of mankind, and it has been superseded by terms such as "minister" or "pastor," which involve only a general, indefinite idea of religious service. And wherever the sacramental idea is held only formally, and without any consciousness of its reality, the term Priest also is held in doubt and with an implied protest, or explained away as a popular confusion of terms. Only in the Catholic communion has the term Priest lived on, indissolubly bound up with the whole cycle of her ministrations, and within the Church only where the deep mystery of her being and her oneness with "the powers of the world to come" are apprehended, does the term carry home to the mind its full meaning and expression.[1]

---

[1] The writer of the article on the term Priest, in the Encyc. Britann., speaking popularly, takes a similar view, as to the application of the term, considering it to be rightly employed in the Church, except by those who, like the Presbyterians, hold the Eucharist to be of "no other moral import than the mere commemoration of the death of CHRIST." "These," he adds, "cannot consider themselves as Priests, in the rigid sense of the word; but only as Presbyters, of which the word Priest is a contraction."

CHAPTER X.

ARGUMENT OF THE EPISTLE TO THE HEBREWS.

THE Epistle to the Hebrews is the only portion of the New Testament in which the question of the Priesthood is fully treated of. It therefore requires special consideration; and the more so, because S. Paul's expressions are not uncommonly brought forward, as if they were opposed to the doctrine which is here advocated.

The argument in the Epistle touching upon the question, is evidently directed against an error at that time prevailing among the Jews, and which is also met and condemned in the Epistle to the Galatians. Generally speaking, the Jews were not unwilling to receive our LORD as a king, and perhaps also as a prophet; they rejected Him as a Redeemer. They were blinded in the belief, that their ceremonial law was sufficient to justify them in the sight of GOD, having entirely lost sight of its typical character, and the reference it bore to the promised MESSIAH. Hence arose their persuasion of the unchangeableness of the Levitical ordinances, and their maddened opposition to a dispensation which involved, as they thought, the ruin of the only ordained means of acceptance with GOD.

Against this error S. Paul urges, that, from the very nature of things, "it is not possible that the blood of bulls or of goats should take away sins" (x. 4); that the fact of the constant repetition of the same sacrifices proves their inherent inefficacy (x. 1, 2, 3), and the succession of a number of dying men, who needed to offer for their own sins as well as for the sins of the people, the worthlessness of their Priests (vii. 23, 28). It was to their Priests and sacrifices, independently of any covenanted relation with CHRIST, that the Jews trusted; and it is in reference, consequently, to the Levitical system in this, its naked aspect, that S. Paul argues. In contrast with this inherently defective dispensation, the Apostle points out the perfect sinlessness of CHRIST (v. 9; vii. 27; ix. 14); the offering up of His own Blood; the impossibility of His dying any more; and the fact of His having entered into the heavens, and taken His seat at the Right Hand of the FATHER, as proving that His offering of Himself was perfectly availing with GOD, eternal and inexhaustible in its effects. (ix. 12, 14, 26, 28; x. 5, 6, 7, 8, 9.)

The conclusion of the argument is, that there is One only true Priest adequate to the wants of humanity, to Whom there can be no successor; and one only Sacrifice for the cleansing of the soul, which can never be repeated, and has no defects to be supplied. The argument excludes the possibility of a Priesthood offering acceptable sacrifices irrespective of the Sacrifice of the Cross, or a fresh immolation of the One true Lamb of GOD. But whether any means were ordained to apply the virtues of the Sacrifice of the Cross, or a new order of Priests to be the agents in administering them, are questions wholly untouched by it. Nor can the fact that the Sacrifice has been offered, be pleaded as an argument against a continued system of mediation to apply its perfected merits, if we accept the prefigurative system as a means of obtaining an interest in its virtues before it was offered. Nor, again, is the session of the Eternal High Priest in the heavens inconsistent with the appointment of a subordinate Priesthood on earth, any more than the existence of One Almighty Ruler in the heavens precludes the existence of subordinate sovereigns on earth, through whom the laws of His government are administered.

It is urged, however, that this doctrine is irreconcileable with certain expressions occurring in the Epistle, such as the following: "By one offering He hath perfected for ever them that are sanctified" (x. 14); and again, "Now where remission of these is, there is no more sacrifice for sins" (v. 18). These words are supposed to imply, that all has been already done to effect a perfect atonement for sin, and that a personal application to the merits of CHRIST suffices for every man's salvation. Such an interpretation, however, proves more than can possibly be intended by the objectors: for if all has been already done that is required to reconcile GOD and man, then it follows that sin is pardoned before it is committed, and that there is no need of prayer, or faith, or any other means of reconciliation. Or, if it be meant that the way of sacrifice alone is excluded, then such objectors ought to show, why the sacrifices of a race of Priests on earth availed to obtain the benefits of CHRIST's Death before He came, but are unavailing for the same end after His coming.

The doctrine of the Sacraments is in truth beyond the scope of the Apostle's argument. He is asserting the worthlessness of the Jewish ordinances, because the Jews still clung to the shadow, when the Living Truth had revealed Himself. We cling to our Sacraments, because they are to us the manifestations and organs of His invisible grace; not substitutes for Him, still less antagonistic to Him; but, as we believe, our only ordained means of union with Him,—His very fulness, of Which through them we partake.

Moreover, the argument touches not the question of a subordinate Priesthood ministering under its own High Priest. The comparison, on which the argument rests, turns only on the High Priest's special ministry. S. Paul contrasts the typical with the One Eternal High Priest, and the annual sacrifice of the Day of Atonement with our LORD's Ascension into the heavens. The argument opens with the announcement; "Seeing, then, that we have a great High Priest, that is passed into the heavens, JESUS the SON of GOD" (iv. 14); and it closes with a repetition of the same momentous truth: "And having an High Priest over the House of GOD, let us draw near with a true heart." (x. 21, 22.) The allusions throughout are to the Jewish High Priest, and to his going into the Holy of Holies with the blood of the one annual sacrifice, which the Apostle shows to have been fulfilled once and for ever by the Ascension of CHRIST into the highest heavens, with His own Blood, "there to appear in the Presence of GOD for us."[1] Now

---

[1] The only two verses in the whole course of the argument which do not distinctly point to the High Priest and the annual offering of the Day of Atonement are—x. 11, and vii. 27, where occur the terms

the offering of the great Day of Atonement to which reference is here made, had a special purpose. It was ordained for the annual purification of the Mosaic system; to cleanse away the imperfections and impurities of the services of the past year; remove the disabilities which had accrued to Priests and worshippers; repair the involuntary breaches of the law, and thus re-initiate the covenant between GOD and His people. (Lev. xvi. 35.) The daily sacrifices and offices thenceforward continued on under the shadow and seal of that annual act of reconciliation; and thus, year by year, the national life was renewed, and the acceptableness of the covenanted people sustained.

S. Paul's argument, while it involves the comparative worthlessness of all human Priesthood and sacrifices, when viewed in themselves alone, has special reference to that One Offering, and directly asserted *this fact*,—that the true Day of Atonement had at length arrived, which would not lose its efficacy, as those of old, with the expiration of years, but was able itself alone to impart to

---

"Priest" and "daily" as applied to the sacrifices. But commentators in general understand the term Priest in these verses to mean the High Priest as the word is often used indifferently in the Old Testament for either one or the other, its meaning in each passage being determined by the context. And the term "daily," or "day by day," (καθ' ἡμέραν,) is explained by Rosenmuller to mean "continually, from time to time," (sæpenumero, quandocunque res postulat.) Most commentators, however, understand the term literally. But in order to reconcile it to the general tenour of the passage, which so clearly alludes throughout to the office of the High Priest, Dindorff observes, that from "Lev. iv. 3, Theodoret, and Maimonides, we learn that the High Priest *every* day offered up a sacrifice for his own sins and those of the people." But καθ' ἡμέραν is evidently opposed to ἐφάπαξ, and thus may simply mean continually, as opposed to "once for all."

all future acts of sacrifice a continually availing power, and to all Priests and worshippers an enduring acceptableness; that, instead of the constant repetition of the mere shadow, conveying an external cleansing, the Substantial Verity of GOD Himself had appeared in the Flesh, pleading with GOD, and had gone up into the true Sanctuary, "the heavenly places not made with hands," there to abide, interceding for us by a continued presentation of His sacrificed Humanity before the FATHER, till He had "perfected for ever" all "them that are sanctified."

The Atonement of CHRIST exhausted the functions of the typical pontiff; but the typical line of subordinate Priests, ministering through the virtue of the High Priest's offering, and ordained as its necessary complement for the daily reconciliation of the people, requires its own proper fulfilment. This conclusion, which is drawn from the types of the Law, coincides also with the voice of prophecy, which, while it spake not of any earthly High Priest to arise in the new covenant, distinctly foretold the continued existence of Priests and Levites. The HOLY GHOST, in Isaiah, after speaking of the glory of GOD "among the Gentiles," and an "offering unto the LORD" being brought "out of all nations," says, "And I will also take of them for Priests and for Levites, saith the LORD." (Isa. lxvi. 21.) So likewise Jeremiah, immediately after the promise of "the Branch of Righteousness to grow up unto David," says; "For thus saith the LORD, David shall never want a man to sit upon the throne of the house of Israel; neither the Priests, the Levites, want a man before Me to offer burnt-offerings, and to kindle meat-offerings, and to do sacrifice continually." (Jer. xxxiii. 17, 18.) And this assurance is again repeated with a yet more solemn testimony; "Thus saith the LORD, If ye can break My covenant of the day, and My covenant of the night, and that there should not be day and night in their season: then may also My covenant be broken with David, My servant, that he should not have a son to reign upon his throne; and with the Levites, the Priests My ministers. As the host of heaven cannot be numbered, neither the sand of the sea measured; so will I multiply the seed of David My servant, and the Levites that minister unto Me." (iv. 10, 21, 22.) Thus the extension and perpetuity of an evangelical Priesthood was bound up with the destinies of the Son of David. The two mysteries are combined, having a perpetual co-existence; the one, GOD Incarnate in the Flesh; the other, an order of Priesthood ministering the fruits of His Incarnation. Like to this twofold Prophecy was the double type preserved in the ark, where the manna and Aaron's rod lay side by side age after age; the one, prefiguring the true Bread from heaven,—the other, the ever-living Priesthood through which that Bread of GOD was to be distributed. And in a similar manner the Prophet Malachi couples together the Eucharistic Offering with the new order of Priesthood; for, after speaking of the "pure offering" to be offered "in every place" among the Gentiles, he proceeds to say, "And He shall sit as a refiner and purifier of silver, and He shall purify the sons of Levi." The Priesthood was to be changed at the coming of the LORD; and, therefore, not the Aaronic priests, but those whom the sons of Aaron foreshadowed, must be here meant. S. John, interpreting Malachi, and completing the chain of prophecy, represents our LORD (Rev. i. 13) as the One High Priest, ever present in the midst, purifying the angels of the seven churches, whilst He wears the vestments of the legal Priesthood, "clothed with a garment down to the feet, and girt about the paps with a golden girdle."[1]

Moreover, the one special sacrifice of the Law, which most closely corresponds with the sacrifice of the Church, testifies to the same truth; for the yearly Passover, out of which the Eucharist arose, was a commemorative sacrifice. The first Passover only was vicarious, saving life when the first-born of the Egyptians were slain. All subsequent Passovers were sacrifices commemorative of that act of redemption. Yet the successive Passovers were equally sacrifices.[2] They were the necessary pledge of the sustained redemption of the Israelites, as the original Passover in "that night of the LORD" had been of their first deliverance; so that whosoever of the chil-

---

[1] See Sermon ix., on "Aaron," in Mr. Isaac Williams' beautiful volume of sermons on "The Old Testament Characters." The Hebrew term *mincha*, used by Malachi to express the "pure offering," though employed in the Levitical law specifically to denote the meat, or vegetable, offering, yet also is used to denote a flesh-offering, as, e.g., that of the lamb. See Gen. iv. 4; 1 Sam. ii. 17; Dan. ix. 21; Ps. cxli. 2.

[2] Holy Scripture thus speaks of the continued Passover, as a sacrifice. Moses, enjoining what should be done in after ages in the continued life of the people, says; "Thou shalt therefore *sacrifice* the Passover unto the LORD thy GOD, of the flock and the herd, in the place which the LORD shall choose to place His Name there." Deut. xvi. 2. And again, in the same chapter, vv. 5, 6. On this account S. Paul, speaking of the continued type being fulfilled, uses the terms "Sacrifice," "Passover," as applied to our LORD. "CHRIST, our Passover, is sacrificed (ἐτύθη) for us." 1 Cor. v. 7.

dren of Israel failed to eat thereof, he was to be "cut off from Israel." (Exod. xii. 15.)

The Passover was moreover a feast upon a sacrifice. Offered in the temple, it was eaten in the house, thus reaching into the recesses of family, as of national life, spreading beyond the precincts of the temple, and penetrating into the inner chamber; a vivid token of the all-pervading and intimate communion of the Real Presence of the Flesh of the true LAMB. The Passover was specially typical of our sacrifice, or rather our Eucharist is a transfiguration of that Sacrifice, arising out of the remains of the last Paschal Supper, as the heavenly Body of the Resurrection will arise out of the remains of the "image of the earthy." And, as in the case of the type, so our successive Eucharists are commemorative renewals of our LORD's Oblation of Himself, and the life of the Church hangs on their continuance, as the means of perpetuating and applying His one great act of redemption.

Moreover, all the types of the Levitical system bear testimony to the universality of a law, that every act of GOD towards man has some earthly expression; that every gift from heaven flows through some significant ministry in the material world. The whole Mosaic code was framed in order to give visible representations of the mystery of CHRIST; "See, saith He, that thou make all things according to the pattern showed to thee in the mount." (Heb. viii. 5.) It is in perfect accordance with this law, impressed in manifold ways on all former dispensations, that the Invisible still has an earthly Body and visible expression, in symbol only of old, but now in living truth,—that as the smitten Rock, "which was Christ," gave forth a stream flowing beside the camp of Israel, till they reached the bourne of all their wanderings, so according to the mystery made known, we may believe, to S. John while he watched the Water and the Blood flow forth from the pierced Side, a Presence and a continued communion of the sacrificed Humanity, extending Itself from the Cross, is the assurance, the solace, and the abiding life, of the Church during its earthly pilgrimage, never to cease, till " the shadows flee away," and He Whom we now behold and adore under veils and symbols along our daily path, at length reveals Himself in His beauty, Face to face, in the beatific Vision, Which will gladden us in " the land that is very far away," from whence there will be no wandering any more for ever.[1]

[1] The early Church looked upon the Water and the Blood, which flowed from the pierced Side of our Lord, as the sources of the Sacraments of Baptism and the Eucharist, which were regarded by them as the extension of the Incarnation.

CHAPTER XI.

REASONS WHY THE TERM Ἱερεύς (PRIEST) IS NOT APPLIED TO THE CHRISTIAN MINISTRY IN THE NEW TESTAMENT.

IT has been shown how the *idea* of a Priesthood reappearing under a new and higher form in the Christian Church, is frequently expressed in the New Testament; how the Holy Eucharist, instituted by our LORD, and forming the groundwork and centre of all Church worship, involves the necessity of a sacerdotal ministry, and how the terms of the Apostolic commission correspond with, while they rise beyond, the commission of the sons of Aaron. The ordinary ancient name of a Priest (ἱερεύς) is not, however, given to the Christian minister in the New Testament, and it is important to consider the reasons which may be supposed to have led to this disuse of the accustomed name.

Before entering, however, upon this fuller view of the subject, it is necessary to set before the mind one important fact.

"It is evident," as the Church of England bears witness, "unto all men diligently reading the Holy Scripture and ancient Fathers, that from the Apostles' time, there have been these orders of ministers in CHRIST's

Church; Bishops, Priests, and Deacons;" (Preface to Ordination Services;) yet of the names used in Scripture to denote the three orders of the ministry, there was in the beginning none specially distinguishing the second order. Presbyter or Elder is never so applied, but is used as a general term applicable to all the three orders alike. S. Peter applies it to himself, "who am also an elder" (1 S. Pet. v. 6). Where it is written, "they sent it (i.e. the relief from Antioch) to the elders by the hands of Barnabas and Paul" (Acts xiv. 30), the Apostles and probably the rest of the Clergy present are meant. Where again, it is said, "They ordained elders in every Church" (Acts xiv. 23), it is generally supposed that both the second and third orders of the ministry are included. The only name which has the appearance of being appropriated to the second order, is Bishop (ἐπίσκοπος), as, e.g., in S. Paul's Epistles to SS. Timothy and Titus, where it occurs contrasted with the deacon. But this usage of the term could not have been intended to obtain currency, for it was soon appropriated to the first order.

Again, with regard to the distinctive functions of the second order, we gather nothing definite from Holy Scripture. Mention is made of the "elders" who "rule well," and "who labour in the word and doctrine" (1 S. Tim. v. 17); but this description only denotes a general spiritual charge. S. Paul's injunctions in the two Epistles already referred to, which treat most fully upon the subject, are wholly of a practical character. Scripture is in truth silent as to the specific ministrations, as well as to the distinctive name, of the second order of the ministry.

The question of the Episcopate is in precisely the same condition. No specific term designates this order in the New Testament, except it be the term, "angel" (Rev. ii., iii.), which soon fell into disuse. It is only from S. Paul's Epistles to SS. Timothy and Titus, that we are able to infer the existence of an order to which special powers of jurisdiction, the guardianship of doctrine, and the transmission of the powers of the ministry by ordination, were entrusted. The Scriptural proof of the Episcopate rests entirely on such inference, and yet on this order depends the grace of Sacraments, the certainty of doctrine, and the government of the Church.

It is much the same with regard to the Diaconate. We first read (Acts vi.) of certain persons being appointed to superintend the distribution of alms. It afterwards appears in the history, that these same persons were also commissioned to preach and baptize. But no name is attached to the order, till in S. Paul's Epistles to SS. Timothy and Titus, that of deacon occurs in connection with it. More commonly the word διάκονος, translated in our version "minister," is applied in a general sense, as to our LORD (Rom. xv. 8), and to the Apostles (1 Cor. v. 1; Eph. iii. 7).

It is evident, therefore, that no argument can be based on the names, which are used in the New Testament to denote the orders of the ministry. Nor, indeed, could it be expected that distinctive names should have been employed, at a time when the ministry had as yet acquired so little definiteness of organisation. The three orders had been called into existence, and the essential ideas of their separate functions were bound up with the Revelation. But the specific terms to denote them, like the forms of the Catholic creeds, the ritual, and other vital portions of the Christian system, were left to be determined as the fitting time arose, by the living action of the Church under the guidance of the HOLY GHOST, or by unwritten tradition from the Apostles. There were, moreover, special reasons why the particular term, ἱερεὺς, should not have been used at the first rise of Christianity; and these reasons we may now consider.

Christianity arose, not as the antagonist of the Mosaic system, but as its inner life, gradually developed under the covering of its external forms. The infant community of Christians in some degree even recognized the Jewish Priesthood. They observed the Levitical Sabbath. S. Paul, at the instance of the rest of the Apostles, "purified himself and was at charges with four men which had a vow upon them." (Acts xxi. 24.) And of all the brethren it is said, "They continued daily with one accord in the temple." (Acts ii. 26.) Evidently the Church in the beginning was led to cling as long as possible to the Holy City, its Temple and its mysteries, as though the same SPIRIT breathed in her, Which had hung weeping over Jerusalem, still yearning, if it were possible, "to gather her children together, as a hen gathereth her brood under her wings." Not until they were violently forced away, did the Apostles and brethren quit their hold of the sacred precincts. It was manifestly not the design of GOD to precipitate the separation, to throw scorn on the ancient faith, to present Christianity to the world as a rival institution, or bring out too prominently at first all the distinctions which were in due season to unfold themselves out of the old institutions, as their hidden meanings, under new forms. To have assumed at once the long-established name of the minister of the Jewish temple, would have been inconsistent with this economy, and must have placed the Gospel immediately in direct and personal antagonism with the Jewish religion; and while the Christian converts frequented the temple services, and received certain ordinances at the hands of the Jewish Priests, must have caused serious heart-burnings and confusion in the minds of both communities. No such objection on the other hand attached to the term, elder, which was employed by the Jews indifferently for all offices of reverence and authority.

There was besides a further object to be attained. The mind of the Jew was to be weaned from the external associations of his ancient faith. How he clung to the mere " letter" of the law, is evident from the whole history of the New Testament. To disengage the substance from the shadow, in which it had been enveloped, and which the popular conscience had mistaken for the substance itself, was of vital importance. But a very little knowledge of human nature shows, how the superstitious and formal, rather than the essential and spiritual, features of a system cling to long established words, and how difficult it is to remove the ideas habitually attached to them, so long as they continue in use. This could hardly fail to have been the case with a term, around which had grown up all the ideas connected with the Levitical covenant. The disuse of the term may therefore be regarded as a merciful provision to facilitate the progress of the Jewish mind to a clearer view of the spiritual realities of the new kingdom.

That such principles operated in the establishment of Christianity, may be concluded from the fact, that a similar destiny awaited the term "Sabbath." Like the term Priest, it is employed no where in the New Testament in reference to Christianity. The case is even stronger with regard to the term Sabbath, than that of Priest. For the observance of holy days, and specifically of the Sabbath Day, is spoken of with positive reprobation, as destructive of the simplicity of faith in CHRIST. "Let no man therefore judge you in meat or drink, or in respect of an holy day, or of the new moon, or of the Sabbath days, which are a shadow of things to come; but the body is of CHRIST." (Col. ii. 16.) And again: "Ye observe days, and months, and times, and years: I am afraid of you." (Gal. iv. 10.) Again, it may seem on a superficial view, from the fourth chapter of the Epistle to the Hebrews, that all sabbatical observances, or days of rest, had passed away with the coming in of a deeper spiritual life, and that the only rest contemplated by the Gospel is the soul's inward repose on CHRIST. Yet coincidentally with this rejection of the term Sabbath, and of holy days and seasons, the Apostles and brethren were observing the LORD's Day: and Passion-tide, Easter, and Wednesdays and Fridays, as days of observance associated with the Betrayal and Crucifixion of our LORD, may be traced up through the dimness of the earliest tradition to the age of the Apostles. In the writings of the Apostolic Fathers the term Sabbath never occurs except in connection with the Jewish apostacy, which was stigmatized by the opprobrious name of "sabbatizing." Later still S. Augustine speaks of the Sabbath, as observed only spiritually, and having its fulfilment in CHRIST.[1] The subsequent history of the two terms similarly coincides. Both rose to life again after a time, and became fixed in the ordinary language of the Church, only the term Priest at a much earlier date than the other. The term, Sabbath, has not been applied to the day of Christian observance until quite modern times.

This remarkable similarity in the usage of these two terms, forms a very strong presumption that the same principle has operated in both cases. While there was danger to be apprehended from Jewish ideas becoming attached to the new system, from mere confusion, or from the appearance of antagonism, the Jewish terms were suspended, though the *ideas* of Priesthood and Sabbath passed into the Christian system. When this danger no longer existed, and the separation of the two systems was complete, the terms themselves were again freely used. The Priesthood and the Sabbath were the two most striking and characteristic features of the Mosaic system, penetrating the whole national life; and if in any case such a safeguard as has been suggested might be expected to operate, it would have been preeminently in these two cases.

Such a change of names, as is here supposed to have taken place, where the inner life of an institution was developed under a new aspect, occurred in other cases, marking, as it would seem, a general law. Thus the Passover survives in Passion-tide and Easter, Pentecost in Whitsuntide, the Feast of Tabernacles in Advent and Christmas.[2]

[1] S. Aug. on S. John i. 18, and v. 20.
[2] "In its spiritual signification, the Feast of Tabernacles prefigured

There was, moreover, a further and yet deeper principle at work in the formation of the Christian Church, tending to the same conclusion. While the characteristic features of the Mosaic system were being discarded, rites which had prevailed in patriarchal times, and remained only in a subordinate position under the Law, were brought prominently forward, and became distinctive marks of Christianity. Baptism, a custom derived from the earliest ages, becomes the outward form of the initiatory sacrament and the instrument of regeneration. The patriarchal sign of "laying on of hands," is raised to be a part of the "foundations" of Christianity. (Heb. vi. 1.) It is only according to this same principle, that the term elder, which had descended likewise from patriarchal times, as an ever honoured designation of paternal rule, is selected to be the appellation of the minister, who in CHRIST has power to beget sons unto GOD, and to feed them with the bread of immortality.

This reference to patriarchal times, so signally characteristic of the Gospel, which is the fulfilment of the promises made before the Law to the Fathers, has a special application to the case of the Priesthood. S.

the time when GOD was to 'tabernacle,' to pitch His tent among the children of men. . . . . . It is said, by Jewish writers, that they had a custom of singing certain songs and hymns to GOD while preparing the booths; one of which was the cxviii. Psalm, 'Hosannah, save now, I beseech Thee, O LORD;' whence the whole preparations and the feast itself came in process of time to be called Hosannas, the exclamation of the people to the Redeemer in the only moment of triumph during His stay on earth. 'Hosanna to the Son of David.' At this feast Solomon's temple was dedicated, and the ark brought into it—both types of CHRIST in His assumption of humanity."—Mather on the Types. Ch. xxviii. "The Gospel of the Jewish Festivals."

Paul expressly declares that the Priesthood was not destroyed, but "changed," at the manifestation of the True High Priest; and the Fathers generally taught, that the change which ensued was, that the new Priesthood arose, not out of the Levitical order, but directly from CHRIST, being formed, like His Priesthood, "after the order of Melchizedek;"[1] the Levitical Priesthood being not its source, but its type or shadow. "Our SAVIOUR JESUS CHRIST," says Eusebius, expressing the prevailing belief, "does even to this present time celebrate sacrifice among men by His ministers after the manner of Melchizedek, for as he, being a Priest of the Gentiles, nowhere appears to have used corporeal sacrifices, but blessed Abraham in bread and wine, in the same manner our SAVIOUR and LORD, and afterwards all priests that derive from Him, performing in all nations their spiritual functions by bread and wine, do express the mysteries of His Body and saving Blood, Melchizedek having foreseen these things by a Divine Spirit, and having used before these images of future things." (Lib. v. De Dem. Evang. c. 3.)

[1] S. Augustine, in the West, taught the same doctrine: as, e.g. in a striking passage in his discourse on the Thirty-fourth Psalm (Serm 1.)

"But there was before, as yet now, the sacrifice of the Jews, after the order of Aaron, with victims of cattle; and that too was a mystery: not yet was the sacrifice of the Body and Blood of the Lamb, which the faithful know, and those who have read the Gospel; which sacrifice is now diffused throughout the whole world. Set then before your eyes two sacrifices, both that after the order of Aaron and this after the order of Melchizedek. . . . . . Therefore was the sacrifice of Aaron taken away, and began the sacrifice after the order of Melchizedek. . . . . . Even the people of the Jews He sent away, and He departed. For they cleaving to the sacrifice after the order of Aaron, held not the sacrifice after the order of Melchizedek, and so lost CHRIST; and the Gentiles began to have Him, to whom He had not before sent preachers."

It was the prevailing conviction, that the bread and wine which Melchizedek brought forth, were first offered in sacrifice, before they were given as food, and were mysteriously connected with the blessing which Abraham received. It accords remarkably with this conviction, that cakes or wafers of " fine flour," and libations of wine, were the ordinary accompaniments of the animal sacrifices of the temple, or substitutes for them, when, on account of poverty, they were excused. When the true Lamb of GOD offered Himself, the animal sacrifices, His forecast shadows, vanished away; but the bread and wine remained. Having been only subordinate features in the Levitical system, though still invested with some peculiar mystery, they were, like other elements of patriarchal religion, exalted, and became the sacramental symbols of the Body and Blood of the Lamb of GOD; the bread and wine still accompanying the atoning Victim, Which is present and offered with them, though invisibly, and in a mystery. That the Levitical name of the Priesthood should not be assumed by the new Priesthood, until the Levitical accidents had been disengaged, and the Jewish, as contrasted with the Christian, accompaniments of the office ceased to be attached to it, is in harmony with the unity of purpose which has pervaded these progressive dispensations.

The various facts here adduced, moreover, afford a strong confirmation of the principle on which the whole idea of sacerdotal mediation and outward religion rests, (Christianity being no exception, but rather a more real expression of it)—viz. that the invisible has a visible form, through which it acts and manifests itself; GOD coming near to man through organs borrowed from the creature. And as in former covenants the

Unseen has assumed a symbolic clothing, suited to the economy of a mere symbolic dispensation, so now throughout the ever-expanding Catholic communion, a mysterious Presence reveals Itself in sacraments of healing and benediction, in Liturgies and silent adorations before the altar,—a real Presence, suited to the economy of the actual Incarnation of GOD, Which only waits the lifting of the veil, to unfold Itself into the fulness of the mystery of a visible Manifestation in the day of His appearing in the glory of His FATHER, with all His holy angels.

CHAPTER XII.

OF THE TERMS 'IMPROPER,' 'SPIRITUAL,' ETC., AS APPLIED TO THE PRIESTHOOD AND ITS SERVICES.

IT is not unusual for those who reject the full teaching of the Church, to admit that the terms 'Priest,' 'sacrifices,' 'mediation,' &c., may be applied to the Christian minister and his services, only with this qualification, that the terms are used in an improper sense. This qualification is correct, and the term 'improper' is rightly so applied, if understood according to the meaning which it technically bears in theology. As employed, however, by the objectors, the term is supposed to be identical with metaphorical or unreal; and thus, while the doctrine of the Priesthood is admitted in words, it is virtually explained away. But the term has its own technical, theological sense, and when thus understood, so far from overthrowing, tends to confirm the conclusions already obtained. Archbishop Usher explains the theological meaning of the term 'improper,' when he says: "To forgive sins, therefore, being thus proper to GOD only, and to His CHRIST, His ministers must not be held to have this power communicated to them, but in an improper sense, namely, because GOD forgiveth by them, and hath appointed them both to apply those means by which He useth to forgive sins, and to give notice unto repentant sinners of that forgiveness. For who can forgive sins but God alone? Yet doth He forgive by them also unto whom He hath given power to forgive, saith S. Ambrose and his followers." (Answer to a Jesuit's challenge, ch. v.) Archbishop Bramhall, though in other language, explains the same distinction. He uses the term 'proper' in its ordinary, not in its technical sense. "To forgive sins," he says, "is no more proper to God, than to work wonders above the course of nature. The one is communicable as the other. The Priest absolves, or to say more properly, God absolves by the Priest. Therefore he saith, 'I absolve thee in the Name of the FATHER, and of the SON, and of the HOLY GHOST.' God remits sovereignly, imperially, primitively, absolutely; the Priest's power is derivative, delegate, dependent, ministerial, conditional." (Protestant Ordination Defended, Part iv. Dis. vii. sec. 3.) The teaching of both these great writers is the same, though the language varies. 'Proper' in Usher is synonymous with 'imperial, primitive, absolute,' in Bramhall; 'improper' with 'derivative, dependent, conditional,' &c.

When therefore the word 'improper' is applied to the Priesthood, it is with the view of marking the derived and dependent character of its commission, in contradistinction to the Priesthood of CHRIST. It expresses the truth taught by the Fathers, and already stated, that CHRIST "is the only High Priest by nature," and that all other Priests are but channels, through which the acts and virtues of His Priesthood pass, as a fountain diffuses its waters along many ducts, or the sun dispenses its central light through many media.

When, again, the Christian sacrifice is said to be 'improperly' so called, it is to show that its efficacy, or acceptableness, is not independent, but relative to the one perfect Sacrifice of the Cross; or rather that it is acceptable only because it is mystically one with that which has been "once for all" accepted.

The term 'spiritual' likewise requires to be explained. As used by objectors to the Church's teaching, it is supposed to imply that the only real sacrifices of Christian men are those of the heart,—prayer, praise, and thanksgiving; and that an external system of worship, as a necessary means of approach to, and communion with GOD, has no place in Christianity. It is evident that this view brings us back to a system of mere natural religion, according to which GOD is to be worshipped in the heart, as the sole altar of sacrifice, according to the dictates of a man's own mind. The Church as the Body of CHRIST, with its objective, external ordinances, ceases to have any reality, and, instead of being a Divine framework and organization, formed to act on individuals as parts of it, and through their covenanted relations with it, resolves itself into a mere aggregate of individuals as independent atoms, each worshipping according to his own inward light. The whole fabric of external religion, as an ordained system between GOD and the soul, instituted and ruled by a living Spirit ever acting through it, which is the only real idea of the Catholic Church, passes away, and nothing but a formal exterior remains, not worth keeping, except as a matter of social propriety and decent order.

Christian sacrifices are no doubt specially characterized in Holy Scripture as 'spiritual;' but by this term it is not meant that the worship of the heart is the only offering of the Christian religion, but that its external ordinances have been raised to a supernatural order by a fuller and more gracious effusion of the HOLY GHOST, which spiritualises all our sacrifices. A corresponding manner of speech in the Old Testament will help us to understand such expressions when used in the New. At the very time when the temple sacrifices were the necessary and only available means of atonement for any offence, Prophets and Psalmists were enjoining the efficacy of the offerings of the heart, as alone pleasing to GOD, and even condemning "sacrifice, as an abomination to the LORD." It is evident that the intention of such expressions, however strong and frequent, was not to do away with, or disparage, the sacrificial system; but only to elevate the conscience of the worshipper to the appreciation of a higher use of those sacrifices, and to counteract the downward tendency to substitute mere mechanical forms for a living faith. A marked instance of this occurs in the 51st Psalm, wherein a special inspiration conspired with the intense yearnings of a burdened conscience, to bring out in a highly poetical mind the strongest possible conception of the need of the inmost heart's communion with GOD in secret confession and prayer; and yet at the same time the availableness and necessity of the temple sacrifices and its ordinances of purification, are by no means lost sight of. While David says: "Thou desirest no sacrifice, else would I give it Thee" (I can offer nothing of myself sufficiently availing); "but Thou delightest not in burnt-offerings" (even these are not in themselves acceptable) : " the sacrifices of GOD are a broken spirit; a broken and a contrite heart, O GOD, shalt Thou not despise," &c.; he was nevertheless at the same time looking with confidence to the lustrations of the Levitical law; "Thou wilt purge me with hyssop, and I shall be clean; Thou shalt wash me, and I shall be whiter than snow;" and he closes his broken-hearted confession with anticipations of a perfect reconciliation with GOD through the offering of the appointed sacrifice : "Then shalt Thou be pleased with the sacrifice of righteousness" (the sacrifice offered with an intelligent faith, and a heart rightly turned to GOD); "with the burnt-offerings and oblations; then shall they bring young bullocks unto Thine altar." When, again, our LORD recalled an expression of the old Prophets to the recollection of the Jews, and applied it to the question of the observance of the Sabbath Day,—"I will have mercy, and not sacrifice,"—He evidently meant not to annul or disparage the fourth Commandment. He was only re-adjusting the terms of the covenant according to its original spirit, and restoring the old connection between outward and inward religion. He said in another place : "These things ought ye to have done, and not to leave the other undone."

Mede (Lib. ii. ch. v.) has shown how the Fathers uniformly taught this same combination of outward and inward religion to be the true idea of Christian worship. He observes : "For this reason the Christian sacrifice is among the Fathers, by way of distinction, called θυσία αἰνέσεως, sacrificium laudis, that is of Confession and Invocation of GOD; namely, to difference it from those of Blood and Incense." He quotes Clemens Alexandrinus, who says that "the sacrifice of the Church is an oration (λόγος), exhaled from sanctified souls," and then explains the words as alluding to "that sacrifice which the Church offered unto GOD, when she presented herself before Him as one Body in CHRIST, by the mystical communication of His Body and Blood." Again, he says, that when the Fathers speak of GOD delighting only in pure prayer, it is always in opposition to "the shedding of blood and smoke of incense." He moreover quotes a passage from Justin Martyr, usually adduced in opposition to this view, in order to show that such interpretation is an error arising from inattention to the entire context: "That prayer and thanksgivings," says Justin, "made by those that are worthy, are the only sacrifices that are perfect and acceptable unto GOD, I also do affirm, for these are the only sacrifices which Christians have been taught they should perform." To which Mede adds: "If you ask where and how, he tells you 'in that thankful remembrance of their food, both dry and liquid, wherein also is commemorated the Passion which the SON of GOD suffered by Himself.' It is a description of the Eucharist, wherein the Bread and Wine were first presented unto GOD, as a kind of first-fruit offering, to agnize Him the Giver of our food both dry and liquid, and then consecrated to be the symbols of the Body and Blood of CHRIST." It was with the view of making this distinction between Christian and heathen sacrifices, that the Eucharist was commonly designated as the "great unbloody sacrifice," or as it was also called "Eucharistic," because our LORD offered it, while He blessed and "gave thanks."

Two conclusions may be gathered from what has been here said. (1.) The idea of personal power in a Priest over the destinies of his fellow-men, is altogether alien to the teaching of the Church. Heathen superstition invested the Priest even with the attributes of Deity, a belief that may partly have arisen from dark intimations of the Incarnation of GOD cast upon the world from primeval tradition. It may be that even the Jew, bringing his offering to the temple, looked not beyond the minister who stood between him and his GOD, thinking that on his will hung the hope of forgiveness. There is always in a degraded state of mind a tendency to attribute to the outward form or instrument the power which is manifested through its means. But notwithstanding such misconceptions, which may have been popularly attached to the idea of Priesthood, the doctrine which the Church proposes to our belief is clear and definite, viz. that the Christian Priest acts only with a delegated authority and under conditions, in the name and person of another, not his own. CHRIST is pleased to connect His operations with the instrumentality of His servant, borrowing the time and outward form of His act from the creature. The ministration of the Priest is true and effectual only for this very reason, that it is not himself, but GOD through him, Who is fulfilling His own promise.

(2.) When Scripture speaks of spiritual sacrifices, such as prayer and praise, being the only true worship of the new covenant, it is not meant to deny the existence of a mediatorial system, intervening between

GOD and the soul, whereby alone ordinarily the virtues of the Atonement are to be obtained; but that this external system is to be used with an intelligent, living faith; that the oblations of the altar, and the ministration of sacraments, are not to be recognised as truly Christian acts, unless accompanied with the offering of the heart, "for GOD is a SPIRIT, and they that worship Him, must worship Him in spirit and in truth."

CHAPTER XIII.

THE CONNECTION BETWEEN THE CHURCH AND THE SYNAGOGUE.

IT has been already observed, that the same theory which represents the Jewish elder as the prototype of the Christian Priest, supposes the worship of the Church to be derived from that of the Synagogue. It becomes necessary, therefore, to enter more fully into the subject, and it will be found, that while there are points of resemblance both with the synagogue and the temple, the worship of the Church, in its most important elements, may be traced up to the latter as its true type, just as the commission of the Christian Priest was symbolised by that of the sons of Aaron.

The sacrificial system is the only part of the worship of the Jews which was expressly ordained of GOD. Human piety, guided by the HOLY GHOST, subsequently added Psalms, which were sung or chanted in the temple, and private devotions to be used by the people who "waited without," during the time of the offering of the sacrifice. Occasionally the Scriptures were read and taught in the temple; but more regular services for religious instruction, as well as for congregational prayer, grew up apart from the temple. The Prophets, in their own homes, or in "the high places," assembled the people together for these purposes. The schools of "the sons of the Prophets" under Samuel, were organized partly in order to perpetuate these subordinate religious services. During the Captivity these services assumed greater prominence; and on the return to the Holy Land the synagogue system extended itself in every town or village of any size, and throughout the congregations of Jews who were scattered abroad.

The synagogue was a most important instrument for keeping alive in the minds of the people a knowledge of their Scriptures, and habits of congregational prayer. But the service of the synagogue was of the simplest possible kind. No means of atonement after sins committed could be found there; no offerings could be made. Prayers and intercessions there offered, had not the assurance of the promises attached to the temple. Not even a blessing could be there given, unless a priest happened to be present. There were not, as has been already stated, ordained ministers to read, preach, and pray. Any person of sufficient learning happening to be present, was invited to officiate for the occasion. In its whole structure and arrangement, the synagogue bespoke its supplemental character. The building was erected in imitation of the temple, with a court and porches. The daily prayers were at nine A.M., and three P.M., when the morning and evening sacrifices were being offered in the temple; and because the remains of the evening sacrifice were left burning all night on the altar, a night service was held in the synagogue. Special services of fast and festival were also appointed, to correspond with the fasts and festivals of the temple. For the acceptance therefore, of the prayers offered in the synagogue, the Jews trusted to their arising simultaneously with the sweet savour of sacrifice and incense ascending from the altars, towards which GOD had promised that His eyes should ever be open, and His ears intent day and night. And this was the meaning of the Jewish maxim, "Preces in synagogâ occupant locum sacrificiorum." To the temple, as to the gate of heaven, the eyes of the Jews turned from all their dwelling-places; for there alone could be found the covenanted means of communion with GOD, or of reconciliation after any breach of their law. The synagogue was valued for the knowledge which was there obtained of the nature and promises of their covenant; but the links that bound them to GOD, and preserved them within the graces of the covenant, were attached to the temple alone.[1]

The services of the Church grew up precisely in the same manner as those of the former dispensation. The Eucharist only was commanded by the LORD, as the Levitical sacrifices alone were prescribed by the Mosaic law. Prayer, the singing of Psalms, and public teaching, were subsequently added and combined with the Eucharistic Office, under the direction of the Apostles. The service of the Christian assemblies, as represented in S. Paul's Epistle to the Corinthians, is evidently an enlargement of that which was first celebrated in the "upper chamber" at Jerusalem. The daily morning and evening prayers were a still later addition. The

---

[1] For the full account of the Temple and Synagogue services, and their relative connection, see Thorndike's "Service of GOD at Religious Assemblies," especially chapters ii., iii., vii., viii.

only difference to be noted in the two cases is, that the portions of Divine service, which among the Jews grew up separately, and became two distinct systems, were in the Church combined, and formed one harmonious whole.

It is not difficult to distinguish what portions of the Church's ministrations correspond respectively with those of the temple, or the synagogue. The ministries of the Eucharist, of Baptism, of Confirmation, of Absolution, of Benediction, &c., as well as the use of the Psalter, as the main standard of devotion, find their prototypes in the temple. The reading of Holy Scripture, preaching, and congregational prayer, though also to be found in the temple, were more specifically within the province of the synagogue. And as among the Jews, the life of the covenant hung suspended on the ministrations of the temple; so in the Church the covenanted means of communion with GOD, the specially ordained channels of communication between heaven and earth, are to be found in those inner ministrations which correspond with those of the Jewish temple. These, therefore, of necessity form the leading and characteristic features of the Church system, the other being its subordinate and supplemental elements.

The same relation which was established between the religious services of the synagogue and temple, operated also in the exercise of ecclesiastical discipline. The cognizance of offences against the Law lay, in the last resort, with the Sanhedrim, of which the priests were a component part. But in all ordinary matters the power of discipline was committed to the rulers of the synagogue, in the same way that the general teaching of the people, though a part of the office of the priest, was practically in the hands of the rabbis. Thus the ministries of the kingdom of GOD were, among the Jews, discharged by three different bodies of men. While the strictly sacerdotal functions were rigidly confined to the line of Aaron, the rabbis were the teachers of the people, and the rulers of the synagogue the executors of spiritual discipline in the congregations. When the Mosaic system expired, its several ministries " returned to Him who gave" them, and were gathered up again into the Person of CHRIST. But they returned to Him only to be transmitted again to other subordinate agents. And in being again committed unto men, they were no longer to be divided; but as they had centred in Himself alone, so He ordained one line of ministry only to represent Him in these His threefold offices. Thus the functions of the Priesthood, of teaching, and of spiritual rule, were included in the Apostolic commission, that as they are one in our LORD, so the unity of the life of the Church might be exhibited by the combination of all spiritual offices in one consecrated order of men, with whom He had promised to be always, " even unto the end of the world."

It has been urged, on the other hand, that Holy Scripture, in contrasting the two covenants, represents the Christian Jerusalem, the Christian Temple, and the Christian Priest to have been removed into the heavens, (Gal. iv. 26; Heb. viii. 1; ix. 24.) And the conclusion intended to be drawn is, that the Church on earth resembles the condition of those Jews who, from distance or other causes, could have no access to the temple, and for whom the services of the synagogue were provided as a substitute; whose worship, therefore, though in communion with what passed within the temple, was not identical with it. They who argue thus forget that the same Scriptures which represent the holy city, the temple, and the Priesthood as having been raised to the heavens, represent also the entire body of the faithful as having been so translated. The Church itself, through CHRIST, is exalted to a supernatural sphere, and not CHRIST alone, or the temple which, by His SPIRIT, He has made His dwelling-place. "*Ye are come* unto Mount Sion, and unto the city of the living GOD, the heavenly Jerusalem." "But GOD . . . hath *raised us up together*, and made us sit together in heavenly places in CHRIST JESUS." "Our conversation (citizenship) *is* in heaven." Distance has no meaning in the things of the SPIRIT. Through CHRIST's Presence pervading the Church, heaven and earth are become really, though mystically, one.

But the Old Testament types supply the most decisive answer to the objection here proposed. It has been already shown how the act of the typical High Priest entering the Holy of Holies was exhausted in the Ascent of the crucified SON of GOD into the heavens, while yet the ministries of the Jewish Priests have their fulfilment in the ministries of the Church, and thus still survive on earth in their antitypes. A similar conclusion is to be drawn from the typical character of the Jewish Temple. S. Paul divides the Tabernacle into two parts, the first and second Tabernacle, or the Sanctuary and the Holiest of all, between which two divisions hung the second vail, which vail symbolized the Humanity of the SON of GOD. He also describes the Holiest of all as the type of the Highest Heavens, into which CHRIST entered, and to which the Church on earth has now access "through the vail, which is His Flesh," which has been rent. It follows that the Sanctuary represents the Church on earth. The contents of the Sanctuary which S. Paul enumerates, confirm this conclusion; it contained the seven-branched Candlestick and the Table of Shewbread, symbolizing respectively the light of the HOLY GHOST, and the Eucharistic Presence, which are gifts to the Church on earth. While therefore the type of the Holiest of all is exhausted, as well as that of the vail which was rent, that of the Sanctuary is being now fulfilled, expanded so as to embrace within its compass the whole earth, and its ministrations, not ceased, nor removed to another sphere, but diffused, as the Prophet Malachi foretold, "in every place," according to the law of a higher life.[1]

Further it has been urged, that the simplicity of the religious services of the early Christians is at variance with the gorgeous ceremonial which characterised the Jewish temple; and an argument has been drawn from

[1] See Heb. ix. 10. It is worthy of note, that even they who reject the mystery of the Church system, yet recognize the symbolic reference of the Sanctuary to the Christian state on earth. Thus Matthew Henry (on Heb. ix. 1) says: "Now of this Tabernacle it is said, that it is divided into two parts, called a first and a second tabernacle, an inner and an outer part, representing the two states of the Church, militant and triumphant, and the two natures of CHRIST, human and Divine."

See also Mather on the Types, c. xxii. Hammond, following more closely Jewish tradition, considers the entire Tabernacle to be the type of the whole world, Heaven being represented by the second or inner, the earth by the first or outer part. (Comment. on Heb. ix. 1.)

Instead of saying that the types of the Holiest place, and the High Priest's entering in are exhausted, it would perhaps, be truer to say that they are being fulfilled in heaven, as the others are being fulfilled on earth. When it is said that they are exhausted, it is only meant as far as our LORD's meritorious sacrifice on earth is concerned.

this circumstance, in opposition to the view here advocated of the Church's system. The question, however, is not as to the comparative simplicity or gorgeousness of the worship of the Church, which is accidental to its real being; but as to the essential elements of which it is composed. Two important points, moreover, ought to be considered in contrasting the primitive forms of the Church's system with what the piety of later ages has sought to realise.

(1.) A persecuted community, constrained to assemble in private chambers, "the doors being shut," or to take refuge in caves and sepulchres, could not develope a splendid ceremonial; scarcely even observe such decent order as natural propriety would suggest. It was never supposed however that GOD preferred poverty of form in the scenes of His immediate Presence. The Patriarchal rites, as being those of a wandering race, were of the simplest character; but as soon as the religion of the elect people had made for itself a settled home, the Tabernacle, and still more notably afterwards the Temple, assumed the utmost richness and solemnity of ritual. In like manner the early Christian Church, fugitive and fearful of hostile intrusion, restricted itself to what was barely necessary for life, its mysteries concealed, its beauty veiled, to avoid profanation or violence, ever in readiness suddenly to move from place to place. But as soon as persecution ceased, immediately according to the same law which had directed the adornment of the typical Church of Israel, the Christian Church also put on "her beautiful garments," and arrayed herself in a state more suited to the Majesty of Him Who had enshrined Himself in her consecrated symbols. Primitive simplicity was not the normal state of the Catholic Church, but a result of circumstances, or rather the forced suspension of a law which only waited the due season for its natural development. The same chapter in which Isaiah foretold, that "the abundance of the sea should be converted," and "the forces of the Gentiles" enter the Church, gives the following assurance: "The glory of Lebanon shall come unto thee, the fir tree, the pine tree, and the box together, to beautify the place of My sanctuary; and I will make the place of My feet glorious." (Isa. lx. 5—13.)

(2.) The second point has been already in part adverted to. Until the Mosaic polity and the Levitical ceremonial law were dissolved, the Catholic Church was purposely withheld from its intended development, in order that the outward structure of the Jewish system might not be suddenly or rudely overthrown. Mede has expressed it as his opinion, that "after the destruction of Jerusalem, it is likely that the Church received no little improvement in ecclesiastical rites and expressions, both because it was the time of the greatest increase, and because, whilst the Jews' polity stood, her polity for its full establishment stood in some sort suspended." (L. ii. c. iv.)

The same law of progressive expansion, which obtains in the growth of the forms of the material world, has characterised the movements of the grace of GOD, a unity of purpose pervading the successive dispensations, so that there should be no violence of rupture between that which preceded and that which followed, but a gentle transition, as of "the shining light, which shineth more and more unto the perfect day."

H

CHAPTER XIV.

THE PRIESTHOOD OF THE PEOPLE.

OUR inquiry has hitherto been confined to the doctrine of the ministerial Priesthood. But the subject would be open to great misconception, and imperfectly understood, unless viewed in connection with the Priesthood which is the inheritance of all the faithful. The two doctrines are not inconsistent, but rather complementary the one to the other, and are essential parts of a mixed, though harmonious, system.

Calvin's doctrine of the Priesthood of the individual Christian was but an exaggeration of one great truth of the Gospel, to the exclusion of another equally important. He destroyed the analogy of faith, not by asserting error, but by denying truth. He erred from want of harmonising in due proportions two doctrines, neither of which can become injurious, except when viewed separately from the other; but both alike suffer, when either the one or the other is denied. Calvin has not merely injured the revelation of GOD by establishing a system founded on a partial view of Holy Scripture; he has caused it to be believed, that the Priesthood of the minister is incompatible with the Priesthood of the people, and, as a natural result of the undue exaltation of the one to the prejudice of the other, has paved the way to a reaction against the very doctrine, to establish which he made so great a sacrifice. For it is observable, that any real idea of the Priesthood vested in the individual Christian is quite as much obliterated from the popular mind, as that of the ministerial Priesthood. Truth denied has avenged itself, and the exaggerated doctrine has fallen in the same pit that was made for its supposed enemy.

The true remedy is not to follow the opposite course, and deny the Priesthood of the people, in order to claim an exclusive right for that of the minister, but to reconcile the two, giving to each its full proportions. That the two Priesthoods co-existed in the typical Mosaic covenant, is an *à priori* argument in favour of a similar combination in the new covenant, which is its true antitype. And when S. Peter (I. ii. 9) applies a passage of the Old Testament to establish the fact of an inheritance of a royal Priesthood being fulfilled in all the disciples of CHRIST, the identity of language tends to prove, in this as in other respects, the unity of purpose pervading both covenants, and the probability of both Priesthoods reappearing in the same harmonious co-operation in the Christian Church. That the two Priesthoods do thus co-exist, will become manifest if we consider the principles on which they are respectively based,—principles lying deep in the relations established between GOD and man, and characterising all Divine dispensations alike.

The groundwork of the ministerial Priesthood has been already fully considered. It rests on the fact that

God is pleased to communicate the fruits of the Atonement, not by direct influence upon the soul, but through outward means and a human agency. No account can be given of this law of the operations of God, except that it is His will; but, as already observed, the law evidently has respect to the transcendent mystery of the Humanity of our Lord being made the medium of communication between God and man.

The Priesthood of the individual Christian is involved in the process of our redemption. The fall of man worked two evils. It depraved man's nature, and it forfeited his capacity for offering to God acceptable service. The remedy of the one evil did not of necessity involve that of the other; for the power of approaching God with acceptable service, is not the right of any creature, however holy. There are two distinct results flowing from the Atonement; (1.) that man is saved from the power of sin and death; and (2.) that, being saved, he has access to the throne of grace. The capacity for offering spiritual sacrifices in Christ Jesus is an endowment of grace, not identical with, but granted in addition to, the gift of a renewed nature. Christ is revealed to us as a Redeemer, and also as an Intercessor. These two fruits of His sacrifice correspond with the two separate gifts of mercy bequeathed in and through Him. Man rises up supernaturally transformed in Christ, and then becomes entitled again to exercise his forfeited privilege of offering his renewed nature and powers in the service of God. This power of offering himself and his gifts to God, constitutes the Priesthood of the individual Christian.

This grace of Priesthood is bestowed in Holy Baptism.

The baptized man is consecrated for ever to the Divine worship and service, by participating, in his measure, in the Priesthood of CHRIST. This consecration is impressed anew, and with increased fulness, in Confirmation, and becomes what has been called an indelible character of the soul. By this the capacity is given both for receiving other Sacraments, and for making offerings and sacrifices acceptable to GOD. And thus it appears how the two Priesthoods mutually co-operate, and are necessary the one to the other. For as the Priesthood of the baptized Christian is bestowed through Sacraments, so the ministration of Sacraments involves the necessity of the ministerial Priesthood. And, on the other hand, without this priestly character in the baptized, the acts of the ministerial Priesthood would be devoid of their intended efficacy.[1]

Both Priesthoods flow directly from CHRIST. He first glorified the FATHER, by offering up in His renewed Manhood a perfect and acceptable obedience; and then, having thus fulfilled all the claims of GOD upon man, He offered Himself up as an Atoning Sacrifice, that He might communicate Himself, and sanctify in like manner all His brethren. Thus in Himself He laid the groundwork of a twofold Priesthood. Every individual Christian shares through Him the power of offering up acceptable service in his own person by virtue of the former; the Christian minister shares through Him the additional power of offering for, and communicating gifts to, his brethren by virtue of the latter.

The main objection felt to the doctrine of the ministerial Priesthood arises from the supposition that it

[1] See the note at the end of this chapter.

causes a man's salvation to rest, not on his own living faith, but on the act of a fellow-creature; thus either diminishing the need of conversion and personal effort, or supplying a false opiate to hearts ever ready to shift the responsibility of their salvation off themselves. The fear, more or less clearly realized, of an exclusive concernment in religion, or a vicarious service of GOD, or a monopoly of access to the throne of grace, being involved in the doctrine, is the cause of the strong prejudice with which it is assailed. Such errors, however, can only have arisen from neglecting to observe the conditions under which the ministerial Priesthood acts. They are at once obviated by considering what has been already said of the typical ceremonial of the Old Testament. According to the terms of the Levitical law, the process of obtaining forgiveness was a complex act, in which the sinner who sought it had as necessary a share as the Priest. There were two parts in the act of sacrifice; one connecting the transgressor with the victim, and the other connecting the victim with the grace of GOD. The transgressor, bringing the victim to the altar, placed his hands on its head, confessing over it his sins, and acknowledging that the victim was substituted in his place, and about to suffer the punishment he himself deserved. The sacrifice was then offered by the Priest, and the appointed ceremonies were observed by him in order to make an atonement for the sin. Both acts were equally necessary before the atonement was complete. It was the concurrence of the two intermediate acts which brought into effect the promised blessing; and neither party in the complex transaction could supply what was lacking in the other.

What the law of Moses here shadowed out in visible representation, the Gospel teaches, when it declares repentance and faith to be essential conditions on the part of the worshipper, in order to render the act of the Priest available for the attainment of its appointed ends. The use of miraculous power in the hand of the Apostles, was made to be dependent on the response of faith on the part of the recipient of the act of mercy. "And there sat a certain man at Lystra, impotent in his feet, being a cripple from his mother's womb, who never had walked; the same heard Paul speak: who stedfastly beholding him, and perceiving that he had faith to be healed, said with a loud voice, Stand upright on thy feet; and he leaped and walked." (Acts xiv. 8—10.) Faith may be said to have given the blessing as well as the words of the Apostle's mouth; but the latter, by the appointment of GOD, were equally necessary as the former.

The same law prevails as to the better gifts which, through the exercise of sacerdotal power, the Apostles were commissioned to impart. "Repent, and be baptized, every one of you in the Name of JESUS CHRIST for the remission of sins, and ye shall receive the gift of the HOLY GHOST,"—is one instance of this combination of the inward condition and the ministerial act. "What doth hinder me to be baptized?" asked the Eunuch; and Philip answered: "If thou believest with all thine heart, thou mayest." (Acts viii. 34.) These conditions on the part of the receiver of Sacraments are as necessary to their due reception, as their administration by the hands of persons duly appointed of GOD. Faith and repentance were required in order to give efficiency to the intervention of the ministerial act, but the ministry was ordained both for the production of the faith and repentance thus required, and for instrumentally conveying to those who possess these graces the promised blessings of the covenant. For "how shall they believe in Him of whom they have not heard? and how shall they hear, without a preacher? and how shall they preach, except they be sent?"[1] Sent to preach, that men may believe; sent, when men do believe, to remit their sins by Baptism, or if they fall back, to reinstate them by absolution and other means of grace; and to preserve and advance them in communion with GOD by the Blessed Eucharist. Thus a mutual concurrence on the part of the worshipper and the Priest, is of the essence of Sacraments; and as no man can ordinarily by an act of his own mind obtain the promised blessing, so neither, without a corresponding fitness in the receiver, can the act of the Priest impart it. By a right understanding of this principle of co-operation, the idea of the abuse of the sacramental system, popularly implied by the phrase, "opus operatum,"[2] is excluded, and the doctrine

---

[1] Rom. x. 15.

[2] The phrase, "opus operatum," rightly understood, is an important guard to the true Catholic doctrine of Sacraments. It is intended to mark the truth, that the grace of Sacraments is the result of their administration by virtue of CHRIST's institution, as opposed to the idea of the recipient's faith being the instrument of appropriation. Moehler thus explains the phrase: "Sacraments confer on us sanctifying grace, as an institution prepared by CHRIST for our salvation; (ex opere operato, scilicet a Christo, in place of quod operatus est Christus) i.e., the Sacraments convey a divine power, merited for us by CHRIST, which cannot be produced by any human disposition, by any spiritual effort or condition, but is absolutely for CHRIST's sake conferred by GOD through their means."—Moehler on Symbolism, Vol. i. p. 289.

of the Priesthood is shown to be perfectly consistent with the cardinal truth of justification by faith.

In the services of the Church the concurrent act of the people is expressed in the response which follows the prayer and act of the Priest. The response of the congregation seals his act as their own by the expression of a concordant will. Thus, in the Eucharistic Service, the prayer of consecration is followed by the 'Amen' of the assembled people: and afterwards, by virtue of this response, the "sacrifice" is spoken of as "*our* sacrifice of praise and thanksgiving," and "*our* bounden duty and service."

It is not therefore by depreciating the value of the sacerdotal act of the minister, which is an ordinance of GOD, that the possible abuse of His mysteries is to be guarded against; but by cherishing a higher view of congregational worship. To suppose the act of the Priest a substitute for their own, is not likely to be the error of those who have tasted the blessedness of a personal communion with GOD. Neither are they who realize the mystery of their own fellowship in the Body of CHRIST, in a condition to stumble at the mystery, not more marvellous, of a fellow-creature sharing His sacerdotal functions. The loss of the due appreciation of the sacredness of the worship of Almighty GOD, and of wonder at a fallen creature being admitted to adore within the sanctuary, is the real cause of insensibility to the virtue and sanctity of the ministerial commission. How can they who value not congregational prayer as a divine expression of the inner life of the Body of CHRIST, appreciate the greatness of a ministry which speaks and acts in the Person of

CHRIST? A state of feeling like that prevailing in the mass of our people, which regards our Church Service only as an opportunity for public instruction, and the sermon as the centre of its life, is incapable of comprehending the mystery either of their own, or their minister's Priesthood. But the living creatures who are "in the midst of the Throne," and cease not, day and night, saying, "Holy, Holy, Holy," understand the mystery of "the four-and-twenty elders clothed in white raiment," who in harmonious concurrence with their cry arise from their seats, and "fall down before Him that sitteth on the Throne, and worship Him that liveth for ever."[1]

NOTE.

The following definition of the term, character, is extracted from an article which appeared in the Ecclesiastic for March, 1863.

"Sacramental character is therefore defined as being, quædam participatio sacerdotii Christi in fidelibus Ejus. The reality of this character consists in the possession of certain powers for communion with GOD.

"The powers may be either passive or active. Passive powers are those by which we are capable of receiving Divine gifts; so that an unregenerate person, although he receives the 'Sacramentum,' or outward sign in the LORD'S Supper, has no capacity for receiving the 'res sacramenti,' which, being of a spiritual nature, requires a spiritual nature in the recipient.

"And as passive powers are necessary for our individual reception of the graces of CHRIST'S Priesthood, so active powers are necessary for us to communicate the graces of that mediation to others.

"This further character, therefore, is what we receive at our ordination, and it is conveyed by the power of the HOLY GHOST. 'Receive ye the HOLY GHOST,' were the original words of ordination by CHRIST, and the words by which we were ordained. The reality of this reception, as something additional to what we possessed before, consists in the communication of powers to do certain acts of Priesthood, in union with CHRIST our great Mediator."

[1] Rev. iv. 8, 10.

CHAPTER XV.

THE CHIEF FUNCTION OF THE MINISTERIAL PRIESTHOOD.

THE question is sometimes asked, What is the chief function of the Ministerial Priesthood? or, in other words, What is the chief supernatural power which, through Holy Orders, is committed unto men? For Holy Orders are, as has been said, sacramental,[1] certain powers derived from the Priesthood of CHRIST being through them communicated to baptized men for the good of their brethren, together with grace for the due exercise of the powers thus conveyed. To compare the value of the several acts of a ministry, which in all its functions is accompanied with the outgoings of the infinite love of GOD, may seem like the attempt of one who would measure the relative depths of the unfathomed sea. But it is natural to man to attribute to all human actions a value proportioned to the ends which they respectively subserve, or the results which they

---

[1] It is not the sacramental character of Holy Orders which our Reformers questioned, but the classing them as a like Sacrament with Baptism or the Eucharist. "We deny not Ordination to be a Sacrament, though it be not one of those two Sacraments, which are 'generally necessary to salvation.'"—Bramhall. Consecration of Protestant Bishops Vindicated. Disc. v. vol. iii. p. 81, Anglo-Cath. Lib.

tend to produce; and under this view a comparison may be instituted between the several functions of the Priesthood.

The judgment formed upon such a comparison will necessarily depend on the theory which we adopt of the ministerial commission. The upholders of the Presbyter view, consistently with their principles, would attribute the chief weight to the acts of ruling and teaching; while in the estimate of those who follow what has been shown to be the view of the Church, these will be regarded only as subordinate acts, instrumental to yet higher purposes. For it is evident that ecclesiastical discipline and religious instruction are but means to prepare the soul for the remission of sins and union with CHRIST; and therefore the administration of Sacraments, through which these blessings are ordinarily vouchsafed, will be esteemed as the highest function of the ministry. On the other hand, according to the supposition which characterises the Presbyter view, that the grace of remission of sins, and of union with CHRIST, depends only on the soul's secret communion with GOD, the administration of Sacraments, which become in this theory mere signs, sinks into a subordinate position. Taking, however, the Church's view of the subject as our guide, the remission of sin in Holy Baptism and Absolution, and the Holy Eucharist, are to be regarded as the chief functions of the Priesthood, or the special powers which, to use the language of the Church, impress an indelible character or seal upon the soul, as in the most intimate manner associating the person exercising them with CHRIST in His ministerial Priesthood. Jeremy Taylor expresses, in his own striking words, this view of the comparative value of the acts of the Christian Ministry: "And certainly there is not a greater degree of power in the world, than to remit and retain sins, and to consecrate the sacramental symbols into the mysteriousness of CHRIST's Body and Blood; nor a greater honour than that GOD in heaven should ratify what the Priest does on earth, and should admit him to handle the Sacrifice of the world, and to present the Same Which in heaven is presented to the Eternal FATHER." (Clerus Domini, Heber's edit. vol. xiv. p. 452, 459.) This judgment of Jeremy Taylor accords entirely with the deliberate decision of the Bishops in the Savoy Conference, already referred to, when they asserted the necessity of the priestly office, because to it, and to it alone, were committed the two ministries of absolution and consecration.

Judging by the same rule,—that the higher the end obtained by the action, the higher will be the value of the act,—it is evident that of the two ministries which are thus distinguished above all others, that of the Holy Eucharist is the more exalted and eventful. For the remission of sins and reconciliation with GOD is not the final end in which the yearnings of the soul find their full repose; this only prepares the way for the yet further blessedness, which alone adequately meets the wants of fallen humanity, that of union with the Eternal GOD through a perfect incorporation into CHRIST. This ultimate end is the special gift of the holy Eucharist; and therefore it follows, that our ministry finds its crowning glory and perfectness of satisfaction, when the assembled hosts of the people of GOD, having been prepared through teaching and prayer and the ministry of reconciliation, for the final act of communion, are gathered around the altar, and, with Angels and Archangels, and the whole company of heaven, the Presence of the LORD descending, and the dread Sacrifice being represented before the everlasting FATHER, through the HOLY GHOST uniting the earthly and the heavenly ministrations, "The Bread of GOD Which cometh down from heaven, and giveth life to the world," is beheld with the eye of an adoring faith, and is distributed "to all them that love His appearing." What remaineth beyond, but the vision of the Blessed, when He, Whom we now behold veiled and in mystery, will manifest His Glory with open Face?

The same conclusion follows as to the surpassing dignity of the Holy Eucharist, if we contrast it with the Sacrament of Baptism. Although in Holy Baptism the grace of a new Divine Nature, and fellowship in the virtues and merits of the Incarnation and Sacrifice of CHRIST, are first imparted, and only an increased and fuller gift of the same incorporation with CHRIST is bestowed in the Holy Eucharist; yet these two Sacraments are not on this account to be classed as of equal dignity. For there is this distinguishing feature in the celebration of the Holy Eucharist, that in it not only is grace given, but the great Sacrifice, through the merits of which all grace is vouchsafed, is, in some deep mystery, therein contained and applied; and not merely do our LORD's virtues and merits flow forth through it and reach the soul, but He therein exhibits before us, really and substantially, though after a heavenly and incomprehensible manner, the very Flesh and Blood from Which life is imparted to the world. It is, therefore, upon this act of our Priesthood that Hooker chiefly dilates, when enumerating its more prominent characteristics, in language which rises even above his usual grandeur of style, he thus expresses the view of the Church as to the special seal or indelible character which the power of this ministry conveys. "The power of the ministry of GOD translateth out of darkness into glory; it raiseth man from the earth, and bringeth GOD Himself down from heaven; by blessing visible elements, it maketh invisible grace; it giveth daily the HOLY GHOST; it hath to dispose of that Flesh which was given for the life of the world, and that Blood which was poured out to redeem souls. When it poureth malediction upon the heads of the wicked, they perish; when it revoketh the same, they revive. O wretched blindness, if we admire not so great power; more wretched if we consider it aright, and notwithstanding imagine that any but GOD can bestow it! To whom CHRIST hath imparted power, both over that mystical body which is the society of souls, and over that natural, which is Himself, for the knitting of both in one (a work which antiquity doth call the making of CHRIST's Body), the same power is, in such, not amiss both termed a kind of mark or character, and acknowledged to be indelible." (Eccles. Pol. lib. v. ch. lxxvii. s. 1.)

That a frail creature, himself sinful, should thus be made a *representative* of CHRIST to the world, and minister that wonderful Sacrament, in which mysteriously and invisibly, His very Body is made to be present, offered, communicated and diffused, would be altogether beyond comprehension, were it not also a part of the mystery of GOD, to glorify Himself in the worthlessness of the instrumentality which He vouchsafes to employ. If we may venture, without irreverence, so far to explain this mystery, it would appear that, it being the will of GOD to employ an outward as well as an inward ministration, the weakest instrument is the fittest, because there is the less possibility of resting in the instrument, instead of going beyond, and rising up to Him Who thereby invisibly works. Even such as Daniel and S. John were overpowered with the transcendent majesty of ministering Angels, and for a while were absorbed in the entranced contemplation of the minister, to the forgetfulness of the Unseen Presence. How much more would this be our case, if Angels were our ministers. But when one who is known to be of like passions and infirmities with oneself, ministers what is manifestly supernatural and miraculous, the mind at once passes from the fellow-creature into the consciousness of the Higher Being, Who is thus revealing Himself through what can be no more than an external form. Such would seem to be the meaning of S. Paul, when seeking to reconcile his disciples to the greatness of the Apostolic commission, he says, "We have this treasure in earthen vessels, that the excellency of the power may be of GOD, and not of us."[1]

The only question which can remain, in order to establish the ministry of the Eucharist as the chief and crowning dignity of the Priesthood, is to make it clear and indisputable, that, upon consecration by the Priest, the Body and Blood of CHRIST become present in the Sacrament; and, being thus, through his ministry, exhibited before GOD and man, are distributed as the

[1] 2 Cor. iv. 7.

Food of life and immortality. This momentous point, on which so much hangs, for a right understanding of the Christian Priesthood, and the true doctrine of the holy Eucharist, can only be determined by the authority of the Church, the true interpreter of Scripture. As the fittest conclusion, therefore, to this chapter, is annexed a short catena of authorities on the point in question, selected from those who have most fully expressed the mind of the English Church as it is embodied in her Eucharistic service.

Bishop Overall. (Additional Notes on the Book of Common Prayer.) "*These holy mysteries with the spiritual food of the most precious Body and Blood,*" &c. "Before consecration we called them GOD's creatures of bread and wine; now we do so no more after consecration, . . . though the bread remain there still to the eye. . . . And herein we follow the Fathers, who, *after consecration,* would not suffer it to be called bread and wine any longer, but the Body and Blood of CHRIST."

Bishop Taylor. (Discourse of Transubstantiation, in Dissuasive from Popery. Vol. ix. p. 99.) "We (the Church of England) say, as they said, CHRIST's Body is truly there, and there is a conversion of the elements into CHRIST's Body; for what, before consecration, in all senses was bread, is, *after consecration,* in some sense, CHRIST's Body."

Bishop Cosin. (Notes on the Book of Common Prayer. First series.) "It is confessed by all divines, that, *upon the words of consecration,* the Body and Blood of CHRIST is really and substantially present, and so exhibited and given to all that receive It; and all this, not after a physical and sensual, but after an heavenly and incomprehensible manner; but yet there remains this controversy among some of them, whether the Body of CHRIST be present only in the use of the Sacrament, and in the act of eating, and not otherwise. They that hold the affirmative, as the Lutherans (in Conf. Sax.) and all Calvinists do, seem to me to depart from all antiquity, which place the Presence of CHRIST *in the virtue of the words of consecration and benediction used by the priest, and not in the use of the eating of the Sacrament,* for they tell us that the virtue of that consecration is not lost, though the Sacrament be reserved for sick persons or other."

Thorndike. (Laws of the Church. Book iii. s. 5.) "It is not here to be denied that all ecclesiastical writers do with one mouth bear witness to the Presence of the Body and Blood of CHRIST in the Eucharist. Neither will any of them be found to ascribe it to *anything but the consecration,* or that to any faith but that upon which the Church professeth to proceed to the celebrating of it. And upon this account, when they speak of the elements, *supposing the consecration to have passed upon them,* they always call them by the name, not of their bodily substance, but of the Body and Blood of CHRIST, which they have become."

Bishop Bull. (Answer to Bossuet.) "We are not ignorant that the ancient Fathers generally teach that the bread and wine in the Eucharist, *by or upon the consecration* of them, do become and are made the Body and Blood of CHRIST."

Bishop Lake. (Sermon on S. Matt. xxvi. 26.) "What good came to the elements by consecration? *Surely much; for they are made* the Body and Blood of CHRIST."

Wheatley. (On the Common Prayer: of the Prayer of Consecration.) "By these (words) the elements are now consecrated, and *so become* the Body and Blood of our SAVIOUR CHRIST."

Bishop Burnet. (Article XXVIII.) "It is not to be denied, but that very early both Justin Martyr and Irenæus thought that there was such a sanctification of the elements, that there was a divine virtue in them; and in those very passages which we have urged from the arguings of the Fathers against the Eutychians, though they do plainly prove that they believed that the substance of bread and wine did still remain, yet they do suppose an union with the elements to the Body of CHRIST, like that of the human nature being united to the divine.

Field. (Of the Church. Append. Part i. vol. iv.) "Touching the manner of this consecration, there is a great variety of opinions; yet all agree in this, that they understand such a mutation and change to be made, that that which before was earthly and common bread, *by the word of institution, the invocation of God's Name* and Divine Virtue, is made a Sacrament of the true Body and Blood of CHRIST, visibly sitting at the Right Hand of GOD in heaven, and yet after an invisible and incomprehensible manner present in the Church; and that the Body and Blood of CHRIST are in the Sacrament, so exhibited and given as spiritual meat and drink for the salvation and everlasting life of them that are worthy partakers of the same. Thus much we doubt not but a thousand and a thousand miracles may confirm."

Nelson. (Festivals and Fasts.) "Q. In what manner was the consecration of the elements of bread and wine performed in the Primitive Church? A. The priest that officiated not only rehearsed the evangelical history of the institution of the Sacrament, and pronounced those words of our SAVIOUR, 'This is My Body, this is My Blood;' but also offered up a prayer of consecration to GOD, beseeching Him that He would send down His HOLY SPIRIT upon the bread and wine presented to Him on the altar; and that He would so sanctify them, that they might become the Body and Blood of His SON JESUS CHRIST, not according to the gross compages and substance, but as to the spiritual energy and virtue of His holy Flesh and Blood, communicated to the blessed elements by the power and operation of the HOLY GHOST descending upon them; whereby the Body and Blood of CHRIST is verily and indeed taken by the faithful in the LORD'S Supper."

Bishop Wilson. (Sacra Privata, Parker's edit. p. 107.) "He then offered Himself to GOD in the symbols of bread and wine, as a pledge of His real and natural Body, which He was just going to offer to GOD for the sins of the world. His sacramental Body was given, offered, before He suffered. It was made His sacramental Body by His Almighty Word; none but GOD could do it. We therefore invoke the HOLY GHOST, one GOD with Him, to make the elements what CHRIST Himself made them—His sacramental Body; it being the Spirit that quickeneth, the flesh profiteth nothing. It is the SPIRIT, i.e., the HOLY GHOST, *sent upon them in the prayer of the priest*, which conveys to us the seed of eternal life."

Nichols. (Book of Common Prayer.) "And so, again, whereas there was a contention *what it was that made a change in the elements;* whether, as the Roman Church would have it, the bare pronouncing of the words, 'This is My Body,' or as some Protestants say, only the prayer to GOD to sanctify them for a spiritual use, our Church has ordered both a prayer to GOD, and also the words of institution, to be repeated."

Knox. (Remains, Vol. ii. On the use and import of the Eucharistic Symbols.) "In a word, appealing to the Apostle, and that universal belief to which he appeals, the commemorative celebration of the Eucharist, as a devotional act, is not that which makes it peculiarly beneficial and venerable; but it is so, because in this ordinance the aliments which CHRIST has appointed become, through His designation and blessing, the direct vehicles of His own divine influences, to capable receivers. Nothing short of this notion would accord with the ascribing of spiritual virtue specially to each visible sign; and what is still more, to each, *not as becoming efficacious through the act of receiving, but as endowed with efficacy through the act of consecration*. For we must observe, it is not the cup of blessing which we *drink*, nor 'the bread which we *eat*,' that are declared to be the Communion of the Blood and the Communion of the Body of CHRIST: but it is said, 'The cup of blessing which we *bless*,' and 'the bread which we *break*,'—clearly indicating that the Eucharistic elements, when once solemnly sanctified according to our LORD's appointment, are to be regarded as being in an inexplicable, but deeply awful manner, the receptacles of that heavenly virtue which His Divine power qualifies them to convey."

Bishop Mant (quoting Archdeacon Yardley, in his Book of Common Prayer). "*After the consecration* of the elements, immediately follows the reception and distribution of them, which continue still in their natural substance of bread and wine, though they are changed in their value and efficacy into the sacramental Body and Blood of CHRIST."

N.B. It is remarkable, that in the last revision of the Prayer Book, the rubric was added, which provides that "*if the consecrated Bread or Wine be all spent before all have communicated, the priest is to consecrate more according to the form before prescribed, beginning at*" the words which express the *act of* CHRIST as He took the Bread and Wine, and not at the commencement of the prayer, "Hear us, O merciful FATHER." The Church of England by this decision has expressed its accordance with the rest of the Western Church, which has always believed the repetition of our LORD's act and words to be the special time and form of consecration. It is supposed by Archdeacon Yardley that the previous prayer, though not repeated, is presumed still to have force, and to concur with the words of institution, in the case of a second consecration.—(See note in Mant's Prayer Book.)

APPENDIX.

The following extracts from English Divines of chief note among us, are selected from among others, to be added to those already adduced in the course of the argument, in proof of the unvarying doctrine of the Priesthood held in the later, as in the earlier, ages of the Church of England.

Bishop Andrewes.

"The ancient Fathers seem to be of one mind that the same form should serve both, (the Jewish and Christian system of government).

"They ground this their opinion upon that they see,

"1. That the synagogue is called the type or shadow, and the Church the very image of the thing. Heb. x. 1.

"2. That God Himself saith of the Christian Church under the Gentiles, that He will take of the Gentiles, and make them Priests and Levites to Himself (Esay lxvi. 21), there calling our Presbyters and Deacons by those legal names.

"And their often interchange and indifferent using of Priest and Presbyter, Levite or Deacon, showeth they presumed a correspondence and agreement between them.

"Thus, then,
Aaron
Eleazar
Princes of Priests   should be   CHRIST,
Priests   answerable   Archbishop,
Princes of Levites   unto   Bishops,
Levites   Presbyters,
Nethinims   Archdeacons,
                                            Deacons,
                                            Clerks and Sextons."

[N.B. The term 'synagogue' is here used in its wider sense, including the entire Mosaic economy.]—A summary view of the government both of the Old and New Testament: among the minor works. Anglo-Cath. Lib., p. 350.

GEORGE HERBERT.

"CHRIST being not to continue on earth, but, after He had fulfilled the work of reconciliation, to be received up into Heaven, He constituted deputies in His place, and these are priests. . . . . . . Out of this charter of the Priesthood may be plainly gathered both the dignity thereof and the duty: the dignity in that a priest may do that which CHRIST did, and by His authority, and as His vicegerent. The duty, in that a priest is to do that which CHRIST did, and after His manner, both for doctrine and life."—Country Parson, Chap. I.

ARCHBISHOP USHER.

"The government of episcopacy is derived partly from the pattern prescribed by GOD in the Old Testament, and partly from the imitation thereof brought in by the Apostles, and confirmed by CHRIST Himself in the time of the New. The government of the Church of the Old Testament was committed to the Priests and Levites, unto whom the ministers of the New do now succeed, in like sort as our LORD's Day hath done unto their Sabbath, that it might be fulfilled which was spoken by the Prophet, touching the vocation of the Gentiles, 'I will take of them for Priests and for Levites, saith the LORD.' (Isa. lxvi. 21.)"—The Original of Bishops, &c. Vol. vii. p. 43. Van Mildert's edition.

BISHOP PEARSON.

"There were various orders under the law in the ancient temple; and there are likewise various orders under the Gospel. Prophecy, uttered indeed during the time of the law, but to be fulfilled in the times of the Gospel, altogether confirms this. For thus it was written in Isaiah (lxvi. 21), 'I will take of them for Priests and for Levites, saith the LORD.' And thus it was fulfilled by CHRIST. For He called to Himself (1.) Apostles, (2.) the seventy disciples. Thus also, as we know, the Apostles did, for they ordained Presbyters and Deacons."—Minor theological works. Vol. i. p. 274.

BISHOP TAYLOR.

"The Christian ministry having greater privileges, and being honoured with attraction of the Body and Blood of CHRIST, and offices serving 'to a better covenant,' may, with greater argument, be accounted excellent, honourable, and royal; although the Church be called a royal 'Priesthood,' the denomination being given to the whole, from the most excellent part, because they altogether make one body under CHRIST the Head, the medium of the union being the priests. . . . . . His people is 'a peculiar people,' the Clergy 'a holy Priesthood,' and all in conjunction and for several excellencies 'a chosen nation.' . . . . . The priests being enumerated distinct from the people, 'the priests of the kingdom,' and 'the people of the kingdom' are all holy and chosen, but in their several manner: the people of the kingdom, to bring or design a spiritual sacrifice, the priest to offer it; or all together to sacrifice; the priest by his proper ministry, the people by their assent, conjunction, and assistance chosen to serve GOD, not only in their own forms, but under the ministrations of an honourable Priesthood."—The Divine institution of the office ministerial. Sec. 9, vol. xiv. pp. 457, 458. Heber's edition.

HERBERT THORNDIKE.

After noticing the two parts of the Bishop's office, (1.) "to rule the Church and (2.) perform Divine service," he proceeds: "So must we inquire the correspondence of the Church with the synagogue in both respects: reflecting from the Bishop and Presbyters, in regard of Divine service to be performed by their hands, upon Aaron and his sons, or the High Priest and the rest; as Jerome hath done before us, writing in these terms (Epist. ad Evangel.): 'What Aaron and his sons and the Levites were in the temple, that let the Bishop, Presbyter, and Deacons challenge to themselves in the Church.' But in respect of government and discipline . . . . we must reflect upon the Sanhedrim, as the same S. Hierome hath done in another place, upon the first to Titus, saying of Bishops in respect of their Presbyters, 'Imitating Moses, who having in his power to be over the people of Israel alone, chose seventy with whom he might judge the people.'" [N.B. The term synagogue is used here, as by Andrewes, in its wider sense. Vitringa, not adverting to this use of the term synagogue, cites Thorndike as in favour of his views.]—The Primitive

Government of Churches, c. viii. s. 4, 5. Anglo-Cath. Lib. vol. i. pt. 1.

Isaac Barrow.

"We may therefore upon these grounds solidly and safely conclude, that this promise—'I will clothe her priests with salvation,—doth principally belong, and shall therefore infallibly be made good, to the Christian Priesthood, to those who in the Christian Church, by offering spiritual sacrifices of praise and thanksgiving, by directing and instructing the people in the knowledge of the evangelical law, by imploring for and pronouncing upon them the Divine benedictions, do bear analogy with, and supply the room of, the Jewish Priesthood.

"From which discourse we may by the way deduce this corollary: that the title of priest, although it did (as most certainly it doth not) properly and primarily signify a Jewish sacrificer (or slaughterer of beasts), doth yet nowise deserve that reproach which is by some inconsiderately (not to say profanely) upon that mistaken ground cast upon it; since the Holy Scripture itself, we see, doth here, even in that sense (most obnoxious to exception) ascribe it to the Christian pastors. And so likewise doth the Prophet Isaiah (lxvi. 21), ... and the Prophet Jeremiah (xxxiii. 18), 'Neither shall the priests the Levites want a man before Me to offer burnt sacrifices, and to do sacrifice continually;' which prophecy also evidently concerns the same time and state of things, of which the Prophet Malachi thus foretells, 'For from the rising of the sun to the going down of the same, My Name shall be great among the Gentiles; and in every place incense shall be offered unto My Name, and a pure offering.'"—Sermon xii. s. ii. on Ps. cxxxii. 16, fol. edit. vol. i.

Daniel Waterland.

"From hence likewise may we understand in what sense the officiating authorised ministers perform the office of proper, evangelical priests in this (the Eucharistic) service. They do it in three ways: 1. As commemorating, in solemn form, the same Sacrifice here below, which CHRIST our High Priest commemorates above. 2. As handing up (if I may so speak) those prayers and those services of Christians to CHRIST our LORD, Who as High Priest recommends the same in heaven to GOD the FATHER. 3. As offering up to GOD all the faithful who are under their care and ministry, and who are sanctified by the SPIRIT. (Rom. xv. 16.) In these three ways the Christian officers are priests, or liturgs, to very excellent purposes, far above the legal ones, in a sense worth the contending for, and worth the pursuing with the utmost zeal and assiduity."—The Eucharist Considered in a Sacrificial View. C. xii. vol. vii. p. 350. Van Mildert's Edit.

Bishop Beveridge.

"When our LORD, therefore, was upon earth, foreseeing that all the Mosaic orders would cease, in course, upon His death, and knowing that His Church could never subsist without some such orders of men set apart for the administration of His Word and Sacraments, before He died, He took care to lay the platform of others, suitable to His own religion. For which purpose, out of the many disciples that followed Him, He first chose twelve Apostles, to whom He gave commission to baptize, to preach the Gospel, and to work miracles for the confirmation of it; and afterwards He sent out seventy other disciples, and gave them power also to preach the Gospel, and cast out devils in His Name. So that He still kept up the same number of orders in His Church, whilst Himself lived, that was in the Jewish Church; for He Himself was truly the High Priest, of Whom they, under the Law, were only types. Then there were the twelve Apostles, answerable to the priests of the second order; and the seventy disciples, resembling the great number of Levites.

"But all this while, we do not read that the Apostles had any solemn consecration to their office during our SAVIOUR's life. It is said, indeed, in S. Mark iii. 14, that He ordained twelve; but the words are, ἐποίησε δώδεκα, He made or appointed twelve to be His Apostles or messengers. But we do not find that He ordained them, so as to confer any sacerdotal power upon them. He promised, indeed, S. Peter, and the rest of the Apostles with him, that He would give them the keys of the kingdom of heaven. But they were as yet in the hands of the Levitical Priesthood; and He would not take them from thence to give them to His Apostles, so long as that priesthood continued in force. But He was no sooner dead, and risen again, but He presently performed His promise. For then, the Levitical priesthood being expired, and by consequence, the keys, which He had before committed to it by His servant Moses, returning in course into His own hands, He then, according to His promise, gave them to His Apostles.

"For upon the same day that He rose again in the evening, His Apostles being met together, He came to them, and said to them, 'Peace be unto you: as My FATHER hath sent Me, even so send I you. And when He had said so, He breathed on them, and saith unto them, Receive ye the HOLY GHOST: whosesoever sins ye remit, they are remitted unto them; and whosesoever sins ye retain, they are retained.'

"'As My FATHER hath sent Me, even so send I you;'

that is, As My FATHER sent Me to preach the Gospel, by anointing Me with His HOLY SPIRIT, even so, after the self-same manner, I send you. 'Receive ye the HOLY GHOST;' at the speaking of which words He breathed upon them, and so issued forth the HOLY SPIRIT from Himself into them; which, as it is an undeniable argument of the SPIRIT's procession from the SON, as well as from the FATHER, so it was the highest and truest consecration of the Apostles that could be, far beyond that of Aaron and his sons. For they were anointed only with material ointment, which was poured upon Aaron's head, and sprinkled afterwards upon his and his sons' garments, together with the blood of the sacrifice. But this was only a type of that HOLY SPIRIT wherewith the Apostles were anointed by our LORD, when He breathed it immediately from Himself into them.

"And now were the keys of the kingdom of heaven, according to the promise before mentioned, given to the Apostles; and therefore our LORD, after He had breathed upon them, saying, 'Receive ye the HOLY GHOST,' presently adds, 'Whosesoever sins ye remit, they are remitted unto them; and whosesoever sins ye retain, they are retained.' Whereby all sacerdotal power was now conferred upon the Apostles, even whatsoever is necessary to the government and edification of the Church, to the world's end."—Serm. ii., on the Institution of Ministers.

RICHARD HOOKER.

Hooker is usually cited as the one great teacher amongst us who deviated from this unbroken line of doctrine, and was willing to adopt the term Presbyter, instead of that of Priest.

It is necessary, however, to consider under what view, and in what sense, of the terms in question, Hooker was prepared to make this concession to the popular clamour of his day.

(1.) It should be remembered that the full designs of the Puritan party were not developed in Hooker's time, and there were still hopes of reconciling them to the Church's doctrine. Hooker, therefore, with others, was disposed to go the greatest lengths of conciliation, in order to remove any possible stumbling-block in the way of peace.

(2.) Whatever term Hooker was willing to employ, it is probable, from the extract quoted in Chap. xv., that he held the full principle and idea of priesthood in the sense in which it has been attempted to be set forth in these pages; for no more striking passage could be selected, out of any ancient or modern divines, to express the priestly character, and powers of the Christian ministry. In another passage, also, (Eccles. Pol. l. vii. ch. v. 7, vol. ii. p. 345, Keble's edit.,) he cites the well-known passage of S. Jerome, which is one of the clearest and fullest testimonies of antiquity to the truth of the doctrine. "And to the end we may understand that these apostolical orders are taken out of the old Testament, what Aaron and his sons and the Levites were in the Temple, the same in the Church may Bishops, and Presbyters, and Deacons challenge unto themselves." If, therefore, Hooker was willing to accept the term Presbyter, to be consistent with himself he must have understood it, as the ancient Fathers, to be in Christian use synonymous with the term Priest.

(3.) When Hooker says "that sacrifice is now no part of the Christian ministry," and again, "It (the Church) hath properly now no sacrifice," and distinguishes between "heathenish and Jewish service" in this respect on the one hand, and Christian service on the other, on this account thinking that the term Priest might be surrendered, we may believe that he used the term in a popular sense, which

Barrow, in the passage above quoted, expresses, of a Jewish sacrificer, or a slaughterer of beasts."

(4.) When Hooker accepts the term Presbyter, it is by no means in the sense of an "elder," as the Presbyterians, and in particular Vitringa, understand it. He uses the term in its sacramental idea of one ordained to convey the graces of the spiritual life, as a natural father the powers of the natural life. On weighing the following passage, it will be evident that Hooker's mind was embracing this enlarged view of the ministry, in its manifold bearings on the supernatural life, and the communications of Divine grace,—thus including all that has been contended for in these pages,— when he recommends the term to our adoption:

"For what are they that embrace the Gospel, but the sons of GOD? What are churches but His families? Seeing, therefore, we receive the adoption and state of sons by their ministry whom GOD hath chosen out for that purpose, —seeing, also, that when we are the sons of GOD, our continuance is still under their care which were our progenitors, —what better title could there be given them than the reverend name of Presbyters, or fatherly guides? ... A Presbyter, according to the proper meaning of the New Testament, is, 'He unto whom our SAVIOUR CHRIST hath communicated the power of spiritual procreation.' Out of the twelve Patriarchs issued the whole multitude of Israel, according to the flesh. And according to the mystery of heavenly birth, our LORD's Apostles we all acknowledge to be the patriarchs of His whole Church. S. John therefore beheld, sitting about the throne of GOD in heaven, four-and-twenty Presbyters, the one half fathers of the old, the other of the new Jerusalem. In which respect the Apostles likewise gave themselves the same titles, albeit that name were not proper but common unto them with others."—Eccles. Pol. b. v. ch. lxxviii. 4. vol. ii. p. 180, Keble's edit.

If Hooker's view of the ministry were to be taken as the standard of interpretation, there would be little room left for controversy as to the name to be employed to designate it. And coupling together his expressed opinions of the Sacraments, and his idea of the ministry, with his known disposition to go the utmost length of comprehension for peace' sake, we may perhaps understand how far he intended to yield in these his words of charity : "I rather term the one sort Presbyters than Priests, because, in a matter of so small moment, I would not willingly offend their ears to whom the name of Priesthood is odious, though without cause." Vol. ii. p. 178.

To these testimonies of divines may be added that of an honoured layman—

ROBERT NELSON.

"Q. How was the Priesthood esteemed among the primitive Christians ?

"A. The primitive Christians always expressed a mighty value and esteem for their Clergy; because they were sensible there could be no Church without Priests, and that it was by their means that GOD conveyed to them all those mighty blessings which were purchased by CHRIST's death.

* * * * * *

"Q. Why are the ministers of GOD called the Clergy ?

"A. Because those who have been peculiarly appropriated to the service of GOD, and devoted to wait at the altar, have always been esteemed GOD's lot and inheritance, which the word signifies in the Greek. Thus GOD says, 'The Levites shall be Mine;' and our SAVIOUR calls the Apostles the gift His FATHER gave Him out of the world. Now though the word at first comprehended the whole body of the Jewish nation, and may in the same sense be attributed to the community of Christians whom GOD has purchased to Himself as a peculiar people; yet this title was afterwards confined to narrower bounds, and distinguished that tribe which GOD made choice of to stand before Him in the administration of holy things; and after the expiration of that economy, was accordingly used to denote the ministry of the Gospel, and those that were invested with the Priesthood in the Christian Church."

www.ingramcontent.com/pod-product-compliance
Lightning Source LLC
Chambersburg PA
CBHW020242170426
43202CB00008B/190